Navigating Trauma Informed
Traffic Safety

Healing BEHIND THE WHEEL

JANELLE MARIE

HEALING BEHIND THE WHEEL
Navigating Trauma Informed Traffic Safety

This publication is intended for informational and educational purposes only. The advice and recommendations provided herein are not a substitute for professional medical, psychological, legal, or financial advice. Readers are encouraged to seek appropriate professional assistance for any personal or specific needs. While every effort has been made to ensure the accuracy of the information presented in this book, the author, publisher, and the Oregon Department of Transportation assume no responsibility for any errors, omissions, or outcomes related to the application of the information provided. The reader assumes full responsibility for any actions taken based on the content of this book.

Copyright © 2024 JANELLE MARIE

All Rights Reserved. No part of this publication may be recorded, stored in a retrieval system, or transmitted in any form or by any means, electronic, mechanical, photocopying, recording, or otherwise, without prior written permission from the publisher.

Paperback ISBN: 979-8-218-46587-2

First Paperback Edition: December 2024
Printed in the United States of America

Cover by: Make Your Mark Publishing Solutions
Layout by: Make Your Mark Publishing Solutions

Dedication

To the dedicated professionals at the Oregon Department of Transportation and the brave first responders who work tirelessly to keep our roads safe. Your unwavering commitment and compassion help heal not only the physical wounds but also the emotional scars left in the wake of every crash. Your work saves lives, restores hope, and ensures that tomorrow is brighter for all of us.

About the Author

Janelle Marie is an accomplished author and traffic safety advocate with a distinguished career dedicated to promoting road safety and educating the community. As the Executive Director of Oregon Impact, Janelle leads initiatives that administer DUII, Distracted Driving, Youth, and Latino Victims Impact Panels. Her impactful work in schools underscores the grave consequences of making poor choices while driving.

Janelle's contributions to traffic safety have been widely recognized. She received a Commendation Medal from the Portland Police Bureau for her efforts in assisting newly arrived immigrant drivers in Oregon. Additionally, her exemplary leadership earned her the Small Non-Profit Award from the North Clackamas Chamber of Commerce, honoring her high-level achievements as an executive who encourages, inspires, and mentors others.

A lifelong resident of Clackamas County, Oregon, Janelle is deeply rooted in her community. She has spent many years volunteering in schools and various community projects. Outside of her professional life, she finds joy in spending time with her family, especially her grandsons Connor, Camden, and Charlie, who keep her on her toes with their boundless energy.

Janelle's dedication to traffic safety and her community is reflected in her writing, where she continues to advocate for safer roads and more informed drivers.

Contents

Introduction ... ix

PART 1: START WHERE YOU ARE

1. Understanding Trauma on the Road ... 1
2. Early Steps Towards Recovery ... 23

PART 2: ACKNOWLEDGE YOUR BODY AND MIND

3. The Body Keeps the Score ... 45
4. Rebuilding Safety and Trust in Driving ... 67

PART 3: FORTIFY YOUR SUPPORT SYSTEM

5. Support Networks and Their Role in Your Recovery ... 89
6. Advanced Coping Strategies ... 109

PART 4: EXPAND AND EMPOWER

7. Lifestyle Adjustments for Sustained Recovery ... 133
8. Navigating Setbacks ... 153
9. Empowering Others: Turning Pain into Purpose ... 173
10. Looking Ahead-Maintaining Momentum and Building Resilience ... 193

Conclusion ... 207
Resource Links & QR Codes ... 211

Introduction

> "There are wounds that never show on the body that are deeper and more hurtful than anything that bleeds."
> —Laurell K. Hamilton

Melissa got in the car, turned the key in the ignition, and the engine roared to life. Her trembling hands and the beads of perspiration on her forehead were proof of inner distress, which she had been trying to mask with deep breaths. Her eyesight began to blur as she was about to step on the accelerator and drive her car out of the garage. She felt as though she was returning to the terrifying circumstances of the fatal night she had the crash.

I will never forget the sound of my screams as I crashed into the guardrail. It was a moment that changed my life—a moment I had a hard time comprehending in the days that followed. The emotional toll was more detrimental than the physical discomfort, which was already rather severe. I discovered that I was staying off the road, staying out of the car, and staying away from everything that might bring up those terrors and fearful memories. I tried everything to get over the sensation that I was broken and would never be the same, but I was unable to do so. She let out a sigh, thinking back to that horrible experience from her past.

However, Melissa was unaware that she was not the only one experiencing this. Studies have shown that car crashes are among the leading causes of post-traumatic stress disorder (PTSD) in the general population. According to the World Health Organization, almost 1.19 million people's lives are cut short due to road traffic crashes, while around 20-50 million suffer non-fatal injuries, with many incurring a disability.

Research shows that around 38.3% of children/adolescents involved in RTA (Road Traffic Accident) suffered from PTSD a month later.[1] The American Psychological Association reports that PTSD, whether resulting from car crashes or natural disasters, can lead to symptoms such as flashbacks, nightmares, and avoidance of certain situations. Moreover, a cohort study found that even minor trauma can lead to significant psychological distress and PTSD symptoms.[2]

A car crash, whether fatal or not, can be traumatizing for both the driver and the affected person. However, sometimes, some wounds are deeper than the scars that show on the body and hurt more than anything that bleeds.

Living with the aftermath of a traumatic car crash can take a toll on your mental health. Many people who have experienced or witnessed a traumatic traffic accident report persistent anxiety and fear of driving, which can manifest as panic attacks, avoidance of driving, or extreme stress in situations that remind them of the trauma. You may be haunted by flashbacks and traumatic memories that disrupt your daily functioning. These memories can be intrusive and overwhelming, making focusing on your daily life difficult.

The trauma can also affect your sense of confidence and independence, leaving you feeling like you do not have control of your life. This can have a ripple effect on all aspects of your life. You may

---

[1] Post-traumatic stress reactions in young victims of road traffic accidents: European Journal of Psychotraumatology: Vol 8, No sup4 (tandfonline.com)
[2] Posttraumatic stress disorder after minor trauma – A prospective cohort study - ScienceDirect

rely on others for transportation, impacting your personal and professional relationships. Moreover, you may be experiencing physical symptoms of stress and anxiety, such as insomnia, muscle tension, an increased heart rate, and more. These symptoms can be debilitating and make it difficult for you to manage your daily routine.

Worst of all, you may withdraw from social activities, academic engagements, and work obligations that require driving. This isolation can exacerbate your mental health challenges and make it difficult for you to connect with others. Therefore, this is the time to take back control of your life, find ways to heal, and set your life free from the grip of trauma and anxiety.

If you are reading this book, I am guessing you might not be here by chance. You have likely been triggered by a recent experience that has left you shaken and seeking answers. Perhaps you are still reeling from the aftermath of a traumatic traffic crash, and the anxiety and fear that have taken over your life are suffocating. Maybe you are someone who has been holding on to the hope of recovery and empowerment, but it has been an uphill battle. Your ongoing fear and anxiety have been eroding your personal, social, and professional lives.

Whatever the cause, I want you to know that you are not alone in your struggles and your search for help. I understand that you're looking for a way to break free from the grip of anxiety and trauma, and I'm here to guide you through that process.

As someone who has been working with people affected by PTSD after RTA, I know that the journey to recovery is unique to each individual. As you begin this journey of recovery, I want to assure you that this book is designed to provide you with the tools and guidance you need to overcome the challenges of trauma.

By the end of the book, you will have:

- Increased understanding and awareness of trauma and its impact, leading to decreased feelings of isolation and of being misunderstood.
- Restored confidence and control.
- Enhanced coping skills.
- Stronger support system.
- Empowerment and advocacy.
- Long-term recovery and well-being.

Throughout this book, you'll be guided by the "SAFE Road Recovery" Framework, which is a comprehensive approach to trauma recovery. This framework is woven throughout the chapters, providing a clear roadmap for navigating the recovery process.

Here is how the book explains the S.A.F.E. road recovery framework in different chapters:

- **S**tart Where You Are—Understand the trauma and take initial steps to cope immediately after the crash—*Chapters 1-2*
- **A**cknowledge Your Body and Mind—recognize and address the physical and psychological impacts of trauma, and start rebuilding trust in driving—*Chapters 3-4*
- **F**ortify Your Support System—Leverage your support networks and integrate advanced coping strategies into your recovery—*Chapters 5-6*
- **E**xpand and Empower—Make lifestyle adjustments, navigate setbacks, empower others, and build resilience for future challenges—*Chapters 7-10*

By applying the principles and strategies outlined in the "SAFE Road Recovery" Framework, you will begin to experience a transformation in your life. Imagine waking up each morning feeling refreshed, renewed, and ready to take on the day without fearing flashbacks of a crash. You will no longer be held back by anxiety and fear but instead filled with confidence and purpose. The small changes in your daily life will eventually lead to a significant transformation in your current life. From being able to drive without feeling anxious or panicked to reconnecting with loved ones and rekindling old hobbies, you will successfully regain your life.

Studies show that some of the major barriers that prevent people from returning to their normal lives after a car crash include supportive needs, adaptation to new situations, seeking information, and transitioning from functional limitations.[3] This book addresses all these concerns and ensures you have everything you need to regain your confidence and get back on the road.

Road accidents can inflict more pain and trauma than there is to the eye. The wounds on the body may heal, but the scars on the mind are often difficult to fade, let alone erase. Having a constant fear or anxiety after suffering or witnessing a car crash is common. I am aware of your struggles in overcoming the fear and trauma that have been preventing you from moving on. You have tried countless methods and strategies, but nothing seems to have worked for long, leaving you feeling like you are stuck in a never-ending cycle of pain and fear and that there is no escape.

But what if I told you that there is a way out?

This book takes an innovative, compelling and practical approach to trauma recovery in traffic safety. It is based on the SAFE road recovery framework and provides practical advice on pushing your fears down and adopting a positive attitude toward getting back on the road.

---

[3] Road Traffic Accident Victims' Experiences of Return to Normal Life: A Qualitative Study - PMC (nih.gov)

This book is not just another addition to your shelf. It is a lifeline, a source of hope and inspiration that will illuminate your path and guide you toward a brighter, more confident future. With its blend of compassion, expertise, the latest information, and practical wisdom, it aims to offer understanding, validation, and empowerment. As you turn its pages, you will feel a sense of resonance and recognition, knowing that you have finally found the right resource to accompany you on your path to healing.

An important thing to keep in mind regarding PTSD is that it can occur in all people of any ethnicity, nationality, or culture and at any age. Approximately 3.5 percent of U.S. adults every year are affected by PTSD. After completing your healing with this book, you will feel like the best version of yourself, like the person you were meant to be all along. It will make you proud of yourself for facing your fears and pushing through the tough times. That is what I want for you—a life filled with hope, purpose, and joy, free from the shackles of anxiety and trauma.

You must remember that having scars on your body is normal as long as you treat them as a reminder of the past and to improve your present and future lives. Let your scars be a sign of your healing, not the pain and trauma you endured. As Benjamin Alire Saenz writes...

"Scars. A sign that you had been hurt.
A sign that you had healed."

Part One

START WHERE YOU ARE

Chapter One

UNDERSTANDING TRAUMA ON THE ROAD

"Trauma creates change you don't choose. Healing is about creating the change you do choose."
—Michelle Rosenthal

Every journey leaves a mark; some scars are just harder to see. After a traumatic car crash, the physical wounds might heal with time, but the invisible scars—the ones on your mind and soul—often persist, influencing every aspect of your daily life. When you look at a car after a crash, you can often see the damage—the dented fender, the cracked windshield, and the broken headlights. However, that is not the only damage done by the crash. A similar situation happens in the human mind, but the damage is not visible to the naked eye. The wounds in the mind leave psychological scars that can impact your life in more ways than you can imagine. These scars often impact your perception of the world, social interactions, and routine behaviors.

John, a commercial truck driver, realized this when he

experienced a severe crash on an icy highway. Although he survived with minor injuries, the psychological impact was more severe than his wounds. He found himself unable to drive his truck again, experiencing panic attacks at the thought. He felt weak and ashamed until he learned about trauma responses and realized his brain was trying to protect him from further harm. At that moment, he realized that every scar on your body tells a story, which might not always be pleasant to hear. However, regardless of how much you dislike them or want to steer clear of them, you cannot cut them out of your life. The only thing you can do is accept the trauma you endured and try to find a solution for it. Acknowledging that these invisible wounds are real is a crucial step in your healing journey.

THE NATURE OF TRAUMA

Trauma is a complex and complicated experience that can have a profound impact on your physical, emotional, and psychological well-being. Some key aspects of the nature of trauma include:

- An event or situation that is overwhelming and beyond an individual's control.
- A perceived threat to your survival, safety, or well-being.
- Disconnection from oneself, others, and the world leads to feelings of isolation, shame, and guilt.
- Impact on the nervous system and brain.
- Trauma can be passed down through generations and cultural heritage.

Trauma is complex, and its impact varies widely from person to person. Understanding these aspects can help approach trauma with compassion, empathy, and effective support.

DEFINITION OF TRAUMA

Trauma refers to "experiences that cause intense physical and psychological stress reactions. It results from an event, series of events, or set of circumstances experienced by an individual as physically or emotionally harmful or threatening and has lasting adverse effects on the individual's functioning and physical, social, emotional, or spiritual well-being.[4]"

In other words, trauma is a deeply distressing or disturbing event. The American Psychological Association defines it as "an emotional response to a terrible event like a car crash, crime, natural disaster, physical or emotional abuse, neglect, experiencing or witnessing violence, the death of a loved one, war, and more.[5]"

Some of the potentially traumatic experiences include natural disasters, car crashes, physical or sexual abuse, and the death of a loved one.

TYPES OF TRAUMA

The trauma resulting from an unpleasant or unexpected event can be described into various types depending on the intensity and causes.

Below is the classification of trauma based on the causes:

Acute Trauma (Type 1 Trauma)

Acute trauma is also sometimes known as Big "T" trauma, which happens after a major, life-threatening, or life-changing event. This

---

[4] A Review of the Literature - Trauma-Informed Care in Behavioral Health Services - NCBI Bookshelf (nih.gov)
[5] Trauma (apa.org)

type of trauma results from a single incident, such as a car crash, a natural disaster, or a violent attack. The event is typically unexpected and can leave the individual feeling shocked and unable to process the experience. The impact of such events is so strong that the affected person develops symptoms only after experiencing the traumatic event once. For instance, people who suffered deadly hurricanes, earthquakes, wars, or major accidents would likely develop lasting stress and trauma from these events.

Some examples of the events leading to acute trauma include:

- Major car crash
- War and Combat
- Surviving a natural disaster
- The sudden or tragic death of a loved one
- Diagnosis of a life-threatening disease

Complex Trauma (Type 2 Trauma)

Complex trauma develops when the body and mind are so overwhelmed after a distinct traumatic reexperience that they find it difficult to come out of the "fight, flight, or freeze" mode. This type of trauma is also known as little "t" trauma, which develops due to the accumulation of comparatively less threatening but highly distressing events over time. This type of trauma does not depend on the magnitude of the event but rather on the frequency of its occurrence. This refers to exposure to multiple traumatic events, often of an invasive, interpersonal nature. It is particularly damaging as it usually involves betrayal by a trusted person or institution. Complex trauma can have profound effects on a person's emotional and psychological health.

The following events can lead to the development of complex trauma:

- Captivity and torture
- Emotional abuse and neglect from trusted people
- Lack of support during life transitions
- Loss of significant relationships
- Divorce and separation
- Discrimination or bullying
- Harassment and microaggressions
- Parentification
- Substance use in the family
- Human trafficking
- Unsafe housing and homelessness
- Chronic neglect
- Separation or abandonment from primary caregivers

Chronic Trauma

This occurs when a person is exposed to prolonged or repeated distressing events. This type of trauma may persist for several weeks, months, or years. The difference between chronic and complex trauma is that chronic trauma is often within the context of a specific relationship.

Several instances of what can cause long-term trauma include:

- Ongoing abuse
- Prolonged domestic violence
- Living in a war zone

The continuous nature of the trauma can make it more difficult for the individual to feel safe or to trust others, leading to the worsening of the symptoms. The impact of trauma extends to the body and brain, which eventually leads to physical and psychological impacts.

PHYSICAL AND EMOTIONAL IMPACTS OF TRAUMA

The impacts of trauma extend to the physical and emotional aspects of your health and well-being. Below is a breakdown of the impacts of trauma on your body and brain. Trauma significantly affects both the brain and the body, often leading to long-term consequences if not addressed properly.

IMPACT ON THE BODY

Following a traumatic event, you could go through the following:

Physical Injuries: Traumatic events often result in physical injuries, ranging from minor cuts and bruises to more severe wounds requiring medical intervention.

Dysregulated Nervous System: The nervous system controls bodily functions and responses to stress. Trauma can lead to a dysregulated nervous system, resulting in symptoms such as chronic pain, gastrointestinal issues, and cardiovascular problems.

Hormonal Changes: Hormones regulate various body functions, including stress responses. Trauma can disrupt hormonal balance, leading to increased levels of stress hormones like cortisol. This can result in sleep disturbances, weight gain, and immune system suppression.

Sleep Disturbances: Individuals may experience difficulties falling asleep, staying asleep, or experiencing restful sleep, leading to insomnia or disrupted sleep patterns.

Other Physical Symptoms: Trauma can manifest in various physical symptoms, including headaches, fatigue, muscle tension, and respiratory problems. Persistent trauma-related stress can contribute to the development of chronic illnesses, such as heart disease, diabetes, and autoimmune disorders.

IMPACT ON THE BRAIN

Before understanding the impact of trauma on the human brain, you must first have an understanding of the key brain parts. They include the following:

- **Amygdala:** The amygdala detects threats and activates the body's fight-or-flight response. Trauma can cause the amygdala to become overactive, resulting in heightened anxiety and a constant state of alertness.
- **Hippocampus:** The hippocampus is involved in processing and storing memories. Chronic trauma can impair the hippocampus's function, leading to difficulties in distinguishing between past and present experiences, which can result in intrusive memories and flashbacks.
- **Prefrontal Cortex:** The prefrontal cortex helps regulate emotions, make decisions, and control impulses. Trauma can reduce the activity of the prefrontal cortex, leading to challenges in emotional regulation, decision-making, and impulse control.

When a person experiences trauma, their brain goes into survival mode. The changes in the different parts of the brain create an imbalance. This imbalance can lead to:

- **Hyperarousal:** A state of increased anxiety where the person feels constantly on edge and alert to potential danger.
- **Intrusive Memories:** Unwanted, distressing memories of the traumatic event that can occur without warning.
- **Emotional Numbing:** A feeling of being detached from one's emotions and surroundings, often as a coping mechanism to avoid pain.
- **Avoidance:** Efforts to avoid reminders of the trauma can lead to significant changes in behavior and lifestyle.

PHYSIOLOGICAL IMPACTS OF A CAR CRASH

Car crashes are one of the most traumatic experiences one can have. Whether you are behind the wheel or on the other side of it, this experience can have various short-term and long-term psychological impacts on you.

The immediate psychological reactions include:

- Shock
- Fear
- Guilt
- Anger
- Sadness

The long-term psychological reactions and impacts include:

- Post-traumatic stress disorder (PTSD)
- Anxiety and phobias
- Depression
- Substance abuse

One of the most significant psychological impacts of road accidents is post-traumatic stress disorder (PTSD). According to a National Institute of Mental Health (NIMH) study, 39.2% of MVA survivors develop PTSD.[6] It is a psychological condition characterized by persistent fear, flashbacks, and avoidance behaviors.

The only way out of the physical and psychological impacts of trauma is to resort to therapy under expert guidance.

THERAPY AND RECOVERY

The common therapy and recovery options utilized for the treatment of trauma include common behavioral therapy. The treatment options involve addressing both the psychological and physiological effects of trauma. Below is a brief overview of the common therapy and recovery methods used for recovering after a traumatic experience. Further details on this topic will be covered in separate chapters.

COGNITIVE PROCESSING THERAPY (CPT)

Cognitive Processing Therapy (CPT) involves talking about the traumatic experience with your therapist and reanalyzing everything

---

[6] Psychiatric Morbidity Associated with Motor Vehicle Accident... : The Journal of Nervous and Mental Disease (lww.com)

to identify the actual cause of the event. When you talk about your traumatic experience and its impact on your life, you gain clarity of thought. Your therapist may ask you to write in detail about your experience to help you examine your actual thoughts about your trauma. They will then focus your attention on the actual factors leading to that traumatic event to make you realize that it was not your fault, as many things that contribute to an event are beyond human control. This clarity of thought and mind helps you accept reality and come out of guilt, preventing you from living your life to the fullest.

COGNITIVE BEHAVIORAL THERAPY (CBT)

Cognitive behavioral therapy (CBT) aims to change your perception of your trauma to help you come out of your stressful emotions. Common CBT techniques used for the treatment of PTSD include cognitive restructuring, stress inoculation training, meditation, and journaling. By talking about your trauma and trying to think about it from different lenses and perspectives, you can get rid of the negative thoughts surrounding your mind and have a fresh perspective on life.

PROLONGED EXPOSURE THERAPY

As discussed earlier, stress can sometimes lead to avoidance, and you tend to evade places, social settings, smells, sounds, or things associated with your traumatic experience. For instance, if you had a horrible car crash in the past, you may avoid driving a car. Prolonged exposure therapy addresses this issue by motivating you to face your fears by engaging in the activities you unnecessarily avoid. Under this treatment method, your therapist teaches you effective mindfulness techniques to help reduce your anxiety around traumatic things and experiences. Gradually, they expose you to the things you have been avoiding by teaching you how to face them. Later on, they may ask you to record yourself talking about your trauma and listen to it to face and accept reality. These expert-guided exercises eventually help reduce your symptoms and improve your overall condition.

EYE MOVEMENT DESENSITIZATION AND REPROCESSING (EMDR)

Unlike other therapy options, eye movement desensitization and reprocessing (EMDR) does not involve talking to your therapist about your trauma. Rather, it involves concentrating on it while watching or listening to what they are doing. For instance, they might be making movements such as moving a hand or leg, flashing a light, making a sound, or moving an object. This exercise aims to divert your attention from a negative experience towards something positive while recalling your traumatic experience. The consistent practice of this exercise gradually leads to improved outcomes.

INTRODUCTION TO TRAUMA-INFORMED CARE (TIC)

Trauma-informed care (TIC) is an approach that acknowledges the widespread impact of trauma and understands potential paths for recovery. It recognizes the signs and symptoms of trauma in clients, families, staff, and others involved within a system. Trauma-informed care seeks to actively resist re-traumatization by integrating knowledge about trauma into policies, procedures, and practices.

Trauma-informed care adopts a more empathetic approach to encourage individuals to share their problems without hesitation. It acknowledges that healthcare organizations and care teams need to have an in-depth insight into a patient's life situation to provide effective, healing-oriented healthcare services. This approach improves patient engagement by building a trust-based relationship and enhancing healthcare outcomes. It can also help reduce avoidable care and excess costs for healthcare and social services.

PURPOSE AND OBJECTIVES OF TRAUMA-INFORMED CARE

The primary purpose of trauma-informed care is to create a safe and supportive environment that promotes healing and recovery for individuals who have experienced trauma. It aims to enhance the quality of care by offering support and care through the following objectives:

To Promote Healing and Recovery: TIC aims to facilitate the healing process by addressing the physical, emotional, and psychological effects of trauma. This involves providing holistic care that meets the diverse needs of trauma survivors.

To Improve Quality of Care: By integrating trauma awareness into care practices, TIC enhances the effectiveness and quality of services provided. This leads to better outcomes for clients and a more supportive environment for staff.

To Enhance Client Engagement: Trauma-informed care seeks to increase the engagement and participation of clients in their own care. When individuals feel safe, respected, and understood, they are more likely to engage fully in their treatment and recovery processes.

To Foster Resilience and Coping Skills: TIC aims to build resilience by equipping individuals with coping strategies and resources that help them manage stress and adversity. This fosters a sense of empowerment and self-efficacy.

To Reduce Stigma and Increase Understanding: Educating staff, clients, and the community about the impact of trauma and the principles of trauma-informed care helps reduce stigma and increase empathy and support for trauma survivors.

PRINCIPLES OF TRAUMA-INFORMED CARE

SAMHSA (Substance Abuse Mental Health Services Administration) has defined six essential principles for adopting a trauma-informed care approach.

1. **Safety:** Trauma-informed care aims to create a physical and emotional environment that feels safe and secure for individuals who have experienced trauma. This includes physical safety, emotional safety, and staff training.
    - **Physical safety:** ensuring the physical environment is free from hazards and threats.
    - **Emotional safety:** creating a calm, predictable, and non-threatening atmosphere.
    - **Staff training:** ensuring staff are aware of trauma's impact and can respond appropriately.

2. **Trustworthiness and Transparency:** TIC builds trust through consistent, empathetic, and open interactions, being transparent about policies and procedures, treatment plans and goals, communication and decision-making processes,

and staff credentials and roles. This transparency strengthens the trust between the caregivers and the trauma survivors.

3. **Peer Support:** A vital principle of TIC is providing support from peers who have experienced similar traumas. This practice fosters a sense of community and connection and builds understanding and empathy among caregivers. It also ignites a spark of hope and resilience among the survivors, which eventually improves outcomes.

4. **Collaboration and Mutuality:** Trauma-informed care involves working together with individuals, families, and communities to develop personalized plans and solutions. It also involves recognizing the equal importance of:
    - Client and provider perspectives
    - Family and community involvement
    - Shared decision-making and goal-setting

5. **Empowerment, Voice, and Choice:** The idea of trauma-informed care is based on the belief that every trauma can be healed. This firm belief leads to the empowerment of the survivors, providing them with their own voice and choice of their preferred treatment methodology.

Peter A. Levine, in his book *Waking the Tiger: Healing Trauma,* defines empowerment as: *"Empowerment is the acceptance of personal authority. It derives from the capacity to choose the directions and executions of one's own energies."*

As trauma survivors, you are already resilient, and trauma-informed care aims to empower you by supporting and enhancing your inner strength. It helps you spot your strengths and abilities that you are unable to see under the clouds of doubt and uncertainty. When you leverage your inner wisdom and strength, empowerment becomes inevitable.

6. **Cultural, Historical, and Gender Issues:** Trauma-informed care actively moves past cultural stereotypes and biases, including the biases built upon race, ethnicity, sexual orientation, age, and geography. It focuses on offering gender-responsive services, leveraging the healing value of traditional cultural connections, and recognizing and addressing historical trauma.

   It involves recognizing and respecting:
   o Cultural differences and values
   o Historical trauma and its ongoing impact
   o Gender identity and expression
   o Intersectionality and how multiple identities intersect

   This includes adapting approaches to address diverse populations' unique needs and experiences and acknowledging the impact of systemic oppression and discrimination.

BENEFITS OF TRAUMA-INFORMED CARE FOR SURVIVORS OF TRAUMATIC CAR CRASHES

The foremost benefit of TIC is reduced symptomology. Trauma-informed care helps reduce the severity and frequency of trauma-related symptoms, such as:

- Flashbacks and nightmares
- Anxiety and depression
- Hypervigilance and an exaggerated startle response
- Self-destructive behaviors and substance abuse
- Suicidal thoughts and behaviors

By acknowledging the trauma's impact, prioritizing safety and comfort, and empowering individuals, trauma-informed care can help reduce the distressing symptoms associated with trauma, leading to improved overall well-being and quality of life.

Here is how trauma-informed care benefits trauma treatment and recovery:

ACKNOWLEDGMENT OF THE TRAUMA'S IMPACT

Trauma-informed care acknowledges the deep impact of trauma on an individual's life, recognizing that their experiences have shaped their behaviors, emotions, and coping mechanisms. This acknowledgment helps individuals feel validated, heard and understood. This proves to be the first step towards healing. When people feel that their experiences are recognized as real and significant, their voices and stories are listened to and respected, and their behaviors and emotions are seen as coping mechanisms rather than weaknesses, they tend to focus on the brighter side of the picture to improve their lives.

PREVENTION OF RE-TRAUMATIZATION

Re-traumatizing is defined as *"one's reaction to a traumatic exposure that is colored, intensified, amplified, or shaped by one's reactions and adaptational style to previous traumatic experiences."*[7] In simpler terms, it refers to reliving or reexperiencing a previous traumatic event. Although re-traumatization does not completely sabotage the recovery process, it can significantly hinder it, along with other consequences. You may lose trust and security, experience feelings of pessimism, intense flashbacks, paranoia, or have increased reactivity to stress as a result of re-traumatization. Therefore, it is crucial to prevent it from happening by seeking trauma-informed care.

A core objective of TIC is to avoid practices and interactions that could re-traumatize individuals. This involves being mindful of triggers and stressors that could cause distress and ensuring that care practices do not inadvertently perpetuate trauma.

ENHANCED SAFETY AND COMFORT

Trauma-informed care prioritizes creating a safe and comfortable environment, reducing the risk of re-traumatization. This leads to:

- Reduced anxiety and fear
- Increased sense of control and empowerment
- Improved trust in providers and services
- Enhanced physical and emotional well-being

By acknowledging the trauma's impact and prioritizing safety and comfort, trauma-informed care creates a supportive environment for individuals to heal, recover, and thrive.

---

[7] PsycNET Record Display (apa.org)

EMPOWERMENT AND AUTONOMY

Trauma-informed care empowers you to take control of your life by making informed decisions about your care and treatment. This leads to increased self-efficacy, autonomy, and self-advocacy. After completing your treatment, you can manage your life and make positive changes. It helps you understand that you can make choices and decisions about your care, free from coercion or manipulation.

As a result, you can break out of your shell and express your needs and preferences, advocating for yourself and your overall well-being.

HOLISTIC AND INDIVIDUALIZED CARE

Through comprehensive treatment plans, trauma-informed care addresses the whole person, considering physical, emotional, spiritual, and social needs. This involves treatment plans tailored to address the individual's unique needs and goals. Moreover, the overall approach to care is adapted to respect and honor an individual's cultural beliefs, values, and practices.

It addresses the trauma's impact by acknowledging the far-reaching effects of trauma and addressing how it affects daily life and relationships.

INTEGRATION OF SUPPORT SYSTEMS

Trauma-informed care combines various support systems, ensuring a collaborative and cohesive approach. This leads to:

- **Interdisciplinary teams:** Professionals from different fields work together, sharing expertise and resources.

- **Family and community involvement:** Loved ones and community members are engaged in the care process, providing emotional support and connection.
- **Referrals and linkages:** Individuals are connected with resources and services, ensuring continuity of care and support.

INCREASED TRUST

Trauma-informed care builds trust between individuals and providers, fostering a safe and supportive relationship. This leads to:

- **Consistent and reliable care:** Providers are dependable and follow through on commitments.
- **Transparency and honesty:** Providers are open and truthful about treatment plans, progress, and challenges.
- **Shared decision-making:** Providers collaborate with individuals, respecting their autonomy and input.

Trauma-informed care creates a supportive environment for individuals to heal, recover, and thrive by prioritizing empowerment, holistic care, integrated support systems, and trust.

COMMON EMOTIONAL REACTIONS TO A CAR CRASH — A CHECKLIST

Car crashes can lead you to feel a rush of different emotions, which, if not identified, may intensify your trauma. Below is a checklist of common emotional, behavioral, physical, and cognitive reactions you may experience after a traumatic car crash. Understanding and acknowledging the reactions to car crashes is a crucial step in recovery. This checklist can help you identify and recognize common emotional, behavioral, physical, and cognitive reactions. Print it and keep it with you in case of an emergency.

Emotional Reactions

- ☐ PTSD
- ☐ Anxiety and fear
- ☐ Depression
- ☐ Anguish and emotional distress
- ☐ Guilt
- ☐ Anger
- ☐ Shock and numbness
- ☐ Fearfulness
- ☐ Avoidance
- ☐ Exhaustion

Behavioral Reactions

- ☐ Social withdrawal
- ☐ Sleep disturbances
- ☐ Changed eating habits
- ☐ Increased consumption of alcohol or drugs
- ☐ Inability to stop focusing on what occurred
- ☐ Turning to substances such as alcohol, cigarettes, and coffee

Physical Reactions

- ☐ Fatigue
- ☐ Nausea and dizziness
- ☐ Headache

- ☐ Excessive sweating
- ☐ Increased heart rate

Cognitive Reactions

- ☐ Reduced concentration and memory
- ☐ Intrusive thoughts
- ☐ Repeated flashbacks of the event
- ☐ Confusion or disorientation.

The following are the guidelines to make the most of this checklist:

- Self-reflect and review each reaction; check off the one that you experienced since the accident.
- Be mindful of the frequency and intensity of these reactions.
- Understand that these reactions are normal and valid trauma responses.
- Share this checklist with a therapist, counselor, or support group.

Recognizing and acknowledging these reactions is a crucial step toward recovery. Filling out this checklist will help you validate your emotions and identify the reactions that are most disruptive to your life. As a result, you can work with your healthcare provider to address and manage these symptoms. Remember, you are not alone and are only a step away from seeking help. This book will guide you through understanding these reactions in more detail and provide strategies to cope with and overcome them.

CONCLUSION

Suffering trauma after a car crash is never a pleasant experience; however, how you respond to it makes all the difference. Use the information and the guidelines discussed in this chapter as a starting point to acknowledge and voice your feelings and experiences. As mentioned at the beginning of the chapter, some scars are invisible but affect you the most. However, if treated right, these scars can surely turn into stars and a symbol of your resilience.

But this does not happen overnight. You must take the first step, regardless of how small it is, toward learning and understanding the multi-layered nature of trauma and its emotional, behavioral, physical, and cognitive dimensions. Besides learning about trauma responses, it is also important to accept your emotions instead of denying them. This is the first step toward healing from your unpleasant experiences and living a better life. This understanding will also prepare you for your next step in the journey, which involves implementing initial coping strategies immediately following an accident to prevent long-term psychological effects.

With every chapter in this book, we will dig deeper into the SAFE Road Recovery Framework, offering actionable insights and tools to empower you to reclaim confidence, resilience, and well-being behind the wheel. I know how exhausting it can be to be constantly at war with yourself. And I also know you are tired of this war and trying to escape this vicious cycle. Remember that things will eventually change, and you will make it through with your consistent efforts. Healing from trauma means showing up for yourself every day. Let me guide you on this transformative journey, where you can heal from your traumas with the power of knowledge and action.

Chapter Two

EARLY STEPS TOWARDS RECOVERY

"Trauma shatters the illusion of invincibility, but in that vulnerability lies the seeds of strength."

—Jayneen Sanders

The first steps in recovery are often the smallest yet the most crucial. In the immediate aftermath of a traumatic event like a traffic crash, your actions can deeply impact your long-term well-being. These initial moments soon after a tragedy are often characterized by clouds of shock and disorientation, which numb your mind, making it difficult to analyze and react to a situation logically. However, during these initial moments of shock and disorientation, your ability to cope effectively can make all the difference in preventing the development of the long-term psychological effects highlighted in the previous chapter.

As some moments pass, the adrenaline subsides, and the reality of what has happened begins to sink in. It is natural to feel overwhelmed and uncertain about what to do next. The mind seems to go blank when it comes to thinking about your next action to cope with the situation. During that time, it is essential to remember that you have the power to take control of the situation, even when you feel stuck amid chaos with no way out of sight. By implementing specific coping strategies in the early stages following the crash, you can cope with the immediate challenges and lay the groundwork for a smoother recovery journey in the days and weeks ahead. As the first step of the SAFE recovery framework entails, start where you are; your early steps towards recovery must begin right after a traumatic experience has occurred.

CASE STUDY

Jane, a 34-year-old marketing executive and mother of two, had a terrible experience driving to the office one day. It was during her kids' summer break when she had to go to the office for an urgent meeting for a crucial project. She was traveling on a gravel road when she had a head-on collision. Her head impacted the post between the windshield and the passenger door, making her lose consciousness for a while. Moments later, she was able to open her eyes but could not move her legs or arms to get out of the car. Her head was spinning, making her vision blurred, but she knew she had to act quickly. She somehow managed to grab her phone and dial the emergency helpline. Her first instinct was to call her home, but she soon realized that it was only her children at home, and informing them would not be useful for her. Trying to keep herself awake, she called the rescue services, which arrived soon after.

Jane felt like the minutes stretched to hours, and her headache and numb legs worsened the situation. Despite initial feelings of shock and disorientation, she managed to follow some critical steps.

She called emergency services, ensured her safety, and reached out to her husband for emotional support. At the hospital, she had to undergo critical surgery and weeks of therapy to get back on her feet. Though the crash affected her life significantly, her quick response not only saved her life but also minimized the potential damage that could have occurred had the rescuers not reached her on time.

Jane's presence of mind saved her life despite the horrific crash she was in and the lengthy medical care and recuperation she had to endure. By keeping her emotions under control and taking immediate steps to seek help, she strengthened her foundation for healing and soon returned to her routine.

COMMON IMMEDIATE RESPONSES TO A TRAUMATIC CAR CRASH

A car crash can result in trauma for anyone involved in it, whether as a driver, passenger, or even a witness. In the moments following a traumatic car crash, it is common to experience a range of intense and immediate reactions. These responses are part of the body's natural defense mechanisms, aimed at protecting you during times of extreme stress. Understanding these reactions can help normalize your experience and encourage you to seek appropriate support.

INCREASED HEART RATE AND RAPID BREATHING

When a traumatic event occurs, the body enters a "fight-or-flight" response mode. This response is controlled by the sympathetic nervous system, which releases adrenaline and other stress hormones to prepare you for a stressful situation. These hormones may cause your heart to pound faster and harder.[8] Studies show that trauma survivors often show elevated heart rates immediately after a traumatic experience, which later stabilize.[9]

This physical reaction prepares your body to either fight the danger or flee from it. The adrenaline rush can also make your breaths quick and shallow, increasing the oxygen supply to your muscles and brain to enhance alertness and readiness.

SHOCK, NUMBNESS, OR DENIAL

Shock is a common immediate emotional reaction to a traumatic event, which may manifest as emotional numbness and denial. Emotional numbness refers to feeling detached or disconnected from your surroundings and emotions. It can serve as a temporary buffer to protect you from the overwhelming impact of the trauma.

You might find it hard to accept that the crash has occurred. Denial can help you cope initially by allowing you to process the event gradually.

DISBELIEF

A traumatic experience can often lead to a surreal feeling and the inability to accept and believe the truth. The crash may feel unreal, as if you are in a dream or watching it happen to someone else. This sense of disbelief is a natural reaction to the sudden and unexpected nature of the event. You may find yourself repeatedly asking, *"Did*

---

[8] Effect of intravenous adrenaline on electrocardiogram, blood pressure, and serum potassium. - PMC (nih.gov)

[9] A Prospective Study of Heart Rate Response Following Trauma and the Subsequent Development of Posttraumatic Stress Disorder | Psychiatry and Behavioral Health | JAMA Psychiatry | JAMA Network

this really happen?" or *"Am I dreaming?"* and struggling to piece together the sequence of events.

FEAR AND ANXIETY

When you are caught in a car crash, immediate panic sets in, making it challenging for you to calm yourself down. In such a situation, a surge of fear and anxiety is common. You might worry about your safety, the safety of others involved, or the potential consequences of the crash. It may also lead to hypervigilance, and you may become excessively alert to potential dangers around you, which can lead to heightened anxiety and difficulty calming down.

ANGER

When the disbelief and panic subside, the frustration and rage settle in. Helplessness can lead to a feeling of anger or a sense of injustice, especially if someone else's negligence caused the accident. You might feel frustrated about the disruption to your life and the harm caused to yourself or your loved ones. Even minor annoyances can trigger intense anger as you process the event and its implications.

CONFUSION AND DISORIENTATION

Soon after the crash, you may experience a mental fog and struggle to think clearly or remember details about the accident. This confusion can be disorienting and add to your distress. It also impacts your decision-making process, as you are unable to analyze things properly. Simple decisions, like whether to call someone or what to do next, may feel overwhelming. The brain's ability to process information and make rational choices can be temporarily impaired.

COPING WITH SHOCK AND DENIAL

Experiencing shock and denial after a traumatic experience is normal; however, letting it persist for too long can be harmful to your well-being. Initially, accepting reality might seem challenging, but you must move on in order to heal. The following are some effective strategies to cope with shock and denial after a traumatic experience:

PHYSICAL AND IMMEDIATE ACTION

In the aftermath of a traumatic car crash, coping with shock and denial is crucial. These responses can cloud your judgment and impede necessary actions. Taking concrete steps can help ground you and initiate the recovery process.

ENSURE SAFETY

First things first, you must ensure your safety by moving to a safer location immediately. If possible, move yourself and others to a safe location away from traffic to prevent further incidents. This could involve moving your vehicle to the shoulder of the road or finding a safe spot on the sidewalk. Once you are out of the crash site, check for injuries. Quickly assess yourself and others for injuries. Even if you feel fine, adrenaline can mask pain and symptoms of injury, so it's important to take a moment to ensure everyone's physical well-being.

It is also crucial to activate hazard lights to alert other drivers on the road. Use your vehicle's hazard lights to alert other drivers of the crash. This can help prevent further collisions and ensure the safety of everyone involved.

CONTACT EMERGENCY SERVICES

Call 911 or ask someone nearby to do it if you cannot access your phone. It is crucial to report the crash to emergency services immediately. Provide them with your location, a description of the crash, and any known injuries. They will dispatch police, fire, and medical services as needed. When the help arrives, try to stay online and update the dispatchers about the situation.

Remain on the phone until the dispatcher tells you it's okay to hang up. Follow their instructions carefully and provide any additional information they request. Contact a family member or friend to inform them of the situation. Having someone aware of the incident can provide additional support and assistance if needed.

SEEK MEDICAL ATTENTION

Whether you have incurred minor or major injuries, it is crucial to get yourself immediately checked by healthcare providers to look for internal wounds and bleeding. Even if injuries seem minor, getting a medical assessment as soon as possible is essential. Internal injuries or shock might not be immediately apparent but can have serious consequences if left untreated.

If you are trained, administer first aid to yourself or others while waiting for emergency services. If not, wait for the medical help to arrive. Sometimes, even simple actions, such as applying pressure to a bleeding wound or stabilizing a potential neck injury, can be lifesaving. Moreover, do not forget to document your injuries. Take note of any pain, discomfort, or injuries for future medical consultations. Documentation can be important for both medical treatment and potential legal actions.

EMOTIONAL AND PSYCHOLOGICAL STRATEGIES

Besides taking the physical steps, you must also consider implementing some emotional and psychological strategies to reduce the impact of the trauma and cope with the traumatic situation better.

TAKE DEEP BREATHS, REDUCE PANIC

Right after a crash, when your heart rate is racing and your breaths are rapid, taking a few deep breaths can work wonders for reducing the panic. Slow, deep breaths can help calm the body's stress response. Breathe in deeply through your nose for a count of four, hold for a count of four, and then exhale slowly through your mouth for a count of four. Close your eyes while breathing to temporarily disconnect from the chaos around you. Repeat this several times to help lower your heart rate and reduce feelings of panic. Once you feel a bit better, focus on your immediate environment by engaging your senses. If possible, describe out loud what you see, hear, and feel around you. This can help anchor you in the present moment and alleviate anxiety.

ACKNOWLEDGE YOUR FEELINGS

When the rushing emotions seem to make your mind numb, try calming them down by acknowledging them. Allow yourself to feel and acknowledge whatever emotions arise, whether they be fear, anger, sadness, or confusion. Recognizing and naming your feelings can help you process them more effectively.

While you acknowledge your feelings, it is essential to avoid self-judgment. Understand that your emotional responses are normal reactions to an abnormal situation. Be kind to yourself and avoid judging your feelings.

USE SIMPLE AFFIRMATIONS

When your brain processes trauma, it may lead to a rush of negative thoughts in your mind. For instance, thoughts like *"I'm worthless," "I'm a disaster,"* and *"I don't deserve good things"* may become a constant in your mind. These thoughts can negatively impact your mood and outlook on life and cause low self-esteem.

The best way to prevent negative thoughts from harming your self-esteem and healing is to replace them with positive affirmations.

- *I am safe now.*
- I can handle this.
- This feeling will pass.
- My life is not over because of a crash.
- My body can heal itself, and so can my brain.
- I will get through this situation.
- I give myself time and permission to heal.

These and several other positive emotions of a similar kind can make a significant difference in healing your trauma and helping you stay calm and centered. Remind and reassure yourself that it is normal to feel overwhelmed and that taking things one step at a time is not only okay but the right thing to do.

LIMIT YOUR EXPOSURE TO THE SCENE

One way to cope with stress is by minimizing your exposure to stressors. If it is safe to do so, limit your exposure to the crash scene. This can help reduce the likelihood of further traumatizing yourself. If possible, move to a quieter and safer location. Moreover, try focusing on immediate needs. Concentrate on immediate, practical tasks that need attention. This can help divert your focus from the overwhelming aspects of the crash.

AVOID MAKING MAJOR DECISIONS

When experiencing trauma, you are not in the right state of mind to make major decisions. Therefore, it is better to delay significant choices and decisions. Your judgment may be impaired in the immediate aftermath of a traumatic event. Avoid making major decisions or changes in your life until you feel more stable and clear-headed.

Moreover, if some decisions are inevitable, seek advice from trusted friends, family members, or professionals to ensure you are making the best choices possible.

CONNECT WITH OTHERS

While stress can make it tempting to isolate yourself and avoid socializing, this is actually the time when you need the support of your loved ones the most. Instead of cutting yourself off from your social circle, reach out to them for support. Contact friends, family, or loved ones to share your experience. Talking to someone who cares about you can provide comfort and a sense of security.

If talking with friends and family does not help, or you wish to get expert advice, consider seeking professional help. If you feel overwhelmed, consider reaching out to a mental health professional for immediate support. Therapists and counselors can offer valuable coping strategies and emotional support.

SEEKING INITIAL HELP: PSYCHOLOGICAL FIRST AID

The term Psychological First Aid (PFA) refers to humane, supportive, and practical assistance to fellow human beings who have recently suffered exposure to serious stressors.[10] It usually involves non-intrusive, practical care and support to assess individuals' needs and preferences and help them connect to information, services, and social supports. It involves careful and active listening without pressuring people to talk. This approach protects people from further harm. Unlike the common misconception, it is not something that only professionals can do, nor does it involve asking individuals to analyze the traumatic event. Rather, it aims to comfort people and help them feel calm.

You need psychological first aid for the following reasons:

- Managing acute stress.
- Having access to social, physical, and emotional support.
- Feeling safe and connected.
- Regaining self-control by being able to help themselves.

Just like you rush for first aid after a physical injury, it is crucial to seek help after a traumatic experience. It involves professional assistance and support from your loved ones.

---

[10] Psychological first aid (who.int)

STAY CONNECTED

Social support is one of the most powerful tools for managing acute stress. After a traumatic event, staying connected with those who care about you is important. Talking about your experience, if you feel comfortable, can help process the trauma and reduce feelings of isolation.

- **Share Your Experience:** Explain what happened, how you feel, and what you need. Expressing your thoughts and emotions can provide relief and help you start making sense of the event.
- **Listen and Receive Support:** Allow your loved ones to offer their support. Sometimes, just knowing that others are there for you can be incredibly comforting. Accept their help and understanding, even if it is just having someone hear you out.
- **Join Support Groups:** Consider joining a support group for trauma survivors. Being around others who have experienced similar events can provide a sense of community and understanding.
- **In-Person or Online Groups:** Look for local support groups or online communities where you can share your story and hear from others who are also in recovery. This shared experience can be very validating and empowering.

Staying in touch with your loved ones provides you with the strength and motivation to push through the hard times and find a way to overcome your anxiety and fears.

PRACTICE SELF-CARE

Taking care of your physical health is integral to managing acute stress and supporting emotional recovery.

- **Engage in Physical Activities:** Physical activity can help reduce stress hormones and increase endorphins, which are natural mood lifters.
- **Exercise Regularly:** Engage in regular exercise such as walking, running, swimming, or yoga. These activities can help improve mood and physical well-being.
- **Simple Movements:** If intense exercise feels overwhelming, start with simple movements like stretching or taking short walks. The key is to keep your body active.
- **Maintain a Balanced Diet:** Eating nutritious food can positively impact your mood and energy levels. Focus on consuming a balanced diet rich in fruits, vegetables, lean proteins, and whole grains. Avoid excessive consumption of caffeine, sugar, and processed foods, which can negatively affect your mood.
- **Stay Hydrated:** Drink plenty of water to keep your body hydrated. Dehydration can exacerbate feelings of fatigue and stress.
- **Establish a Sleep Routine:** Try to maintain a regular sleep schedule by going to bed and waking up at the same time each day. Create a calming bedtime routine to help signal to your body that it is time to sleep.
- **Create a Restful Environment:** Ensure your sleeping environment is conducive to rest by keeping it dark, quiet, and cool. Consider using earplugs, an eye mask, or white noise to improve sleep quality.

SEEK PROFESSIONAL HELP

Sometimes, stress becomes so overwhelming that the self-help strategies do not seem to work well. In such situations, professional assistance may be ideal. Know your tolerance point and understand when you need to consult mental health professionals to cope with stress and other conditions resulting from prolonged trauma. Depending on your situation and needs, seeking professional help may involve therapy or consultation.

Engaging with mental health professionals is a critical step in addressing trauma.

- **Therapists and Counselors:** Licensed therapists and counselors are trained to help individuals process trauma and develop coping strategies.
- **Individual Therapy:** One-on-one therapy can provide a safe space to explore your feelings, understand the impact of the trauma, and work through distressing emotions and memories. Common therapeutic approaches include cognitive-behavioral therapy (CBT), which can help reframe negative thoughts and reduce anxiety, and eye movement desensitization and reprocessing (EMDR), which is specifically designed to treat trauma.
- **Group Therapy:** Group therapy offers the opportunity to share experiences with others who have gone through similar events. It can foster a sense of community and provide mutual support and understanding.
- **Psychiatrists:** If needed, consulting a psychiatrist can be beneficial, especially if medication is required to manage symptoms of anxiety, depression, or PTSD.

- **Medication Management:** Psychiatrists can prescribe medications such as antidepressants or anti-anxiety drugs to help manage severe symptoms. Medication can be a helpful tool in conjunction with therapy to provide relief from acute distress.

Remember that there is nothing wrong with asking for help and contacting professionals when needed. In fact, prioritizing your mental well-being is crucial and symbolizes self-love and care.

USE AVAILABLE RESOURCES

If you look around yourself and do some research, you can explore a treasure trove of worthwhile resources available for trauma survivors. Below is a breakdown of resources you can utilize when you have survived or witnessed an accident or when you have caused the crash.

- *When You Have Survived or Witnessed a Crash*

    Crisis Hotlines: Many organizations offer crisis hotlines that provide immediate support and guidance. These services can be a lifeline in moments of acute distress.

    Online Resources: Websites and online platforms offer a wealth of information, self-help tools, and access to virtual support groups. Organizations such as the American Psychological Association (APA) and the National Institute of Mental Health (NIMH) provide valuable resources and directories to find professional help.

Local Mental Health Services: Many communities have local mental health services that offer counseling, therapy, and support groups. Check with your local health department or community centers for available resources.

- ***When You Have Caused the Crash***

    Specialized Therapy: It is crucial to seek therapy to address feelings of guilt, shame, or self-blame. Therapists can help navigate these complex emotions and work toward self-forgiveness and understanding.

    Support Networks: Join support networks specifically for individuals who have caused crashes. These groups can provide a non-judgmental space to share experiences and receive emotional support from others who understand what you are going through. They also facilitate learning to ensure safe driving in the future.

JOIN COMMUNITY AND SUPPORT GROUPS

Community and support groups play a vital role in recovery by providing emotional support, shared experiences, and a sense of belonging. You can find various in-person and online support groups for trauma survivors. These groups offer a platform to connect with others who have experienced similar trauma and seek inspiration from their healing journeys.

Many organizations and community centers offer support groups specifically for trauma survivors. These groups provide a space to share your story, gain insights from others, and receive emotional support. You can also join online communities if you are uncomfortable socializing in person. Online support groups and forums allow you to connect with others from the comfort of your home. Websites like Reddit, Facebook groups, and specialized forums for trauma survivors can provide a sense of community and ongoing support.

Besides joining support groups, consider making the most of community resources for enhanced healing. Local community centers often provide resources such as counseling services, support groups, and wellness programs. These centers can be a valuable source of information and support. Many religious and spiritual organizations also offer support groups and counseling services. These can provide comfort and community support for individuals of faith.

ACTION STEPS FOR THE FIRST 24 HOURS POST-CRASH

The initial hours after a car crash are crucial. You must be highly careful about your action steps and ensure that you are taking essential steps to recover from the accident. Below is a checklist of the necessary action steps for the first 24 hours post-accident.

A CHECKLIST FOR INITIAL ACTION STEPS POST CAR CRASH

Print and keep a copy of this checklist in case of emergency.

Ensure Safety and Assess Injuries
- ☐ Check for injuries
- ☐ Move to a safe location

Contact Authorities
- ☐ Report the accident

Document the Scene
- ☐ Take photographs
- ☐ Exchange information

Seek Medical Attention
- ☐ Visit a healthcare provider
- ☐ Mental health check

Notify your Insurance Company: Contact your insurance company to report the accident. Provide them with all the necessary details and documentation. Follow any specific instructions they give you regarding the claim process.

Self-care and Monitoring
- ☐ Rest and recuperate
- ☐ Monitor symptoms

Legal Consultation: Consult a lawyer to understand your rights and obligations following the crash. Discuss any potential legal claims you might have, especially if there are disputes about fault or if you have sustained significant injuries.

Support System: Rely on your close loved ones for emotional support.

Follow-up on Treatment: Follow any treatment plans your healthcare provider prescribes, including physical therapy and mental health treatment if needed.

Reflect and Learn: Reflect and Learn: Take time to reflect on the crash, your response, and the lessons learned. Implement safety measures in your driving routine to prevent future accidents.

CONCLUSION

What you do to recover from a traumatic experience matters the most and can make a significant difference to the outcomes of your recovery. Usually, we tend to become so consumed in the aftermath of a traumatic experience, such as a car crash, that we waste precious time by not taking the steps that we should take.

The initial steps after a trauma define the course of the recovery and significantly impact the overall healing outcomes. By ensuring your safety, seeking immediate help, and taking care of your physical and emotional well-being in the aftermath of a crash, you can lay the foundation for a long-term recovery. These initial actions help manage the immediate shock and stress, prevent the development of chronic symptoms, and set you on the path to healing.

Once you develop a strong foundation for healing and recovery, you can understand and manage the somatic experience of trauma and how trauma can manifest physically in your body. The next chapter focuses on the various physical symptoms that can arise from psychological stress and trauma, such as muscle tension, headaches, fatigue, and other bodily reactions. It also includes effective methods to address these physical manifestations, including relaxation techniques, physical therapies, and mind-body exercises. Understanding the interconnectedness of mind and body in recovery will enable you to tackle trauma from all angles, facilitating a more holistic healing journey.

Part Two

ACKNOWLEDGE YOUR BODY AND MIND

Chapter Three

THE BODY KEEPS THE SCORE

"I'm still coping with my trauma, but coping by trying to find different ways to heal it rather than hide it."

—**Clemantine Wamariya**

Your body remembers what your mind tries to forget. From traumatic car crashes to injuries affecting your life, your body tends to reminisce about the unpleasant experiences in your life that you want to cut off from your life. Each ache, twinge, and moment of tension in the body speaks volumes about the impact of the event. You may have wondered if it would be possible to simply remove the painful memories of traumatic experiences from your life. Let me break it to you.

No, it is not possible to simply eliminate such memories as if they had never happened. It is because even if the mind tries to forget, the body sometimes finds ways to recall your traumas. However, it does not mean that all hope is lost. Trying to push unpleasant memories often results in exacerbating their intensity. The right approach is to deal with the somatic and psychological impacts of trauma and not let them take hold of your life.

UNDERSTANDING SOMATIC SYMPTOMS

The term somatic symptoms refers to the physical manifestation of the psychological impacts of a traumatic experience. The American Psychiatric Association defines somatic symptom disorder as *"when a person has a significant focus on physical symptoms, such as pain, weakness, or dizziness, to a level that results in major distress and/or problems with daily activities."*[11]

An individual suffering from somatic symptoms disorder has an excessive focus on somatic symptoms, such as injuries from a traumatic experience. For instance, someone involved in a car crash may develop excessive worries about the injuries resulting from the experience and may feel physical impacts such as pain and fatigue. Somatic symptoms are real, tangible physical symptoms that are often linked to emotional or mental health issues. People experiencing somatic symptoms might feel pain, fatigue, or other bodily sensations without an identifiable medical cause.

The major difference between somatic and psychological trauma symptoms is that somatic symptoms refer to the physical manifestations of psychological distress, whereas psychological symptoms include the mental and emotional aspects.

---

[11] Psychiatry.org - Somatic Symptom Disorder

SOMATIC SYMPTOMS OF A TRAUMATIC CRASH

The common somatic symptoms of a traumatic car crash include the following:

Headache and Dizziness

After a traumatic traffic crash, individuals often experience persistent headaches. These can be tension headaches resulting from stress and anxiety, or they may be migraines triggered by the trauma. Additionally, whiplash or other physical injuries to the neck and head during the accident can cause prolonged head pain.

Besides headaches, you may feel lightheadedness, loss of balance, or faintness. These symptoms fall under the umbrella term dizziness. Dizziness may stem from concussions or other head injuries sustained during the crash. It can also be related to anxiety and the body's stress response, which can affect balance and equilibrium. Sometimes, dizziness can be a sign of whiplash or neck strain caused by sudden extension or bending.

Nausea

Another common somatic symptom after a traumatic crash is feeling nauseous. You may feel like throwing up, and your head may be spinning. This condition can occur as a result of the body's physical response to the intense stress and shock of being involved in a car crash. Moreover, sometimes, the injuries sustained during the crash can also lead to nauseous feelings. Nausea can occur immediately following the trauma due to shock and the body's acute stress response. Long-term, it can be a chronic issue linked to anxiety, post-traumatic stress disorder (PTSD), or ongoing stress. The body's heightened state of alertness can affect the digestive system, causing persistent feelings of nausea.

Heightened Startle Response

A traumatic crash can lead to exaggerated reflexes. After a traumatic event, the body's nervous system can become hypersensitive. The heightened startle response, or "jumpiness," means that even minor, non-threatening stimuli can provoke an intense reaction. It is a common symptom of PTSD, where the person remains in a state of hyperarousal. It usually happens whenever you think excessively about the traumatic experience, leading to increased anxiety. It can persist long after trauma, causing you to get triggered and react to anything that reminds you of your trauma.

Trouble Sleeping

Insomnia and nightmares are common after a traumatic experience. Sleep disturbances such as difficulty falling asleep, staying asleep, or experiencing restless sleep can become a part of the lives of trauma survivors. Nightmares about the accident can cause frequent awakenings and contribute to insomnia. The stress and anxiety related to the trauma can make it hard to relax enough to sleep soundly.

Muscle Tension

The jerks and jolts resulting from the crash can lead to chronic pain in different parts of the body. However, pain can also result from psychological distress. The body often holds tension in response to stress and trauma, leading to chronic muscle tension. This is especially common in the neck, shoulders, and back areas. This tension can cause persistent pain and discomfort, further affecting the individual's quality of life.

Hypervigilance

Hypervigilance is characterized by an ongoing sense of being on high alert against potential threats. This means that you may be continuously scanning your environment for potential threats and unable to relax. This state of constant readiness can be exhausting, contributing to stress and anxiety, and is a sign of post-traumatic stress disorder (PTSD). Despite being a psychological condition, hypervigilance can also have physical symptoms, including dilated pupils, elevated blood pressure, and a higher heart rate.

Physical Reactions to Triggers

Crash-induced trauma can lead to trigger-induced responses. Encountering reminders of the accident can provoke intense physical reactions. Triggers might include sights, sounds, or smells similar to those experienced during the accident. Physical reactions can include sweating, shaking, rapid heartbeat, and difficulty breathing, all of which are part of the body's fight-or-flight response.

Understanding these somatic symptoms can help in recognizing and addressing the physical manifestations of psychological trauma following a traffic crash, leading to more effective treatment and recovery strategies.

TECHNIQUES OF PHYSICAL RELIEF

Somatic symptoms can have a significant impact on your life and disrupt its various aspects. To lead a normal life and heal your trauma, you must first focus on seeking physical relief.

SOMATIC EXPERIENCING

Somatic Experiencing (SE) is a therapeutic approach developed by Dr. Peter Levine that focuses on addressing the physiological effects of trauma. It aims to release the trauma stored in the body and restore the natural balance of the nervous system. Somatic experience therapy focuses on creating body awareness while shifting the focus from stressful thoughts and emotions resulting from trauma.

Here are three key techniques used in Somatic Experiencing:

1. **Resourcing:** Resourcing involves identifying and accessing internal and external resources that provide a sense of safety, support, and comfort. It involves calming yourself down and focusing on creating a safe and calming state within yourself. This technique helps you build resilience and create a foundation of stability from which you can safely process traumatic experiences.

   For instance, your somatic therapist may ask you to describe how you might be feeling at a given time. You have to answer it while focusing on and highlighting the positive feelings around you. You may focus on the following internal and external resources to seek inspiration for positivity:

- **Internal Resources**: These might include positive memories, personal strengths, and bodily sensations that are soothing and grounding.
- **External Resources:** These can be supportive relationships, pets, favorite places, or objects that bring peace and security.

During therapy, the practitioner helps you focus on these resources, enhancing your sense of safety and strength before addressing traumatic memories.

2. **Titration:** The second stage of the somatic experiencing techniques involves a procedure called titration. Titration involves gradually and carefully approaching traumatic memories and sensations in small, manageable doses rather than overwhelming you with the entire experience. This technique aims to prevent individuals from becoming overwhelmed by the intensity of their trauma, allowing for safe and gradual processing.

   - The therapist helps the person to gently touch the edges of the traumatic experience, just enough to feel a small portion of the distress.
   - The therapist closely monitors your physical and emotional responses to ensure they remain within your "window of tolerance." It refers to the optimal zone for processing without becoming overwhelmed.
   - By processing the trauma in small doses, you can effectively integrate the experience and build tolerance over time.

3. **Pendulation:** Pendulation refers to the process of shifting attention between states of distress and states of relative comfort and safety to build tolerance. This technique helps you learn to move fluidly between states of discomfort and ease, enhancing your ability to regulate your emotions and bodily sensations. Just as a pendulum moves from one point to another in a to-and-fro motion, this technique involves transitioning between resourcing and titration to develop endurance.

   It usually involves the following steps:

   - The therapist guides you to notice and experience sensations of distress or discomfort associated with the trauma.
   - They then shift your attention to sensations of comfort, safety, or neutrality, often using resources identified earlier.
   - This back-and-forth movement helps discharge the traumatic energy stored in the body and restore balance to the nervous system.

   By practicing pendulation, you can develop greater resilience and a sense of control over your emotional and physiological states.

GROUNDING TECHNIQUES

Grounding techniques focus on pulling you away from the flashbacks and unpleasant memories of the trauma. This helps to suppress feelings of anxiety and stress. Grounding techniques are broadly classified into two categories, namely physical and mental grounding.

1. **Physical Grounding:** The physical grounding techniques involve using your five senses to move from your trauma by connecting to the present moment and the physical environment.

   Some common physical grounding techniques involve the following:

   - **5-4-3-2-1 Technique:** Identify five things you can see, four things you can touch, three things you can hear, two things you can smell, and one thing you can taste. This technique engages all five senses to bring awareness to the present. For instance, look around the room and name five different objects, feel the texture of your clothing, listen to the sounds around you, notice any scents, and savor a piece of gum or candy.
   - **Grounding through Touch:** Use tactile sensations to anchor yourself in the moment. Hold an object such as a stress ball, run your hands over a textured surface, or splash cold water on your face. Feeling the sensation of the object or water helps bring your focus to the present.
   - **Body Awareness:** Focus on the sensations in different parts of your body to ground yourself. Place your feet flat on the floor, and notice the pressure and contact with the ground. Slowly tense and then relax different muscle groups, starting from your toes and moving up to your head, paying attention to how each muscle feels.
   - **Movement:** Engage in physical activities to help ground yourself. Take a short walk, do some light stretching, or practice yoga poses. Physical movement can help redirect focus from distressing thoughts to bodily sensations.

2. **Mental Grounding:** The mental grounding techniques use mental distractions to redirect your thoughts away from distressing experiences to the presence of a peaceful environment. These techniques involve using cognitive strategies to stay connected to the present moment and divert attention away from distressing thoughts or memories.

Some of the most common mental-grounding techniques include the following:

- **Counting Backwards:** Count backward from 100 by sevens or threes. Start at 100 and subtract seven repeatedly (100, 93, 86, 79, etc.). This requires focus and helps divert your mind from distressing thoughts.
- **Describing Your Environment:** Mentally or verbally describe your surroundings in detail. Look around and describe the objects, colors, shapes, and textures you see. For example, *"I see a red chair with four legs, a smooth wooden table, and a blue wall with a picture frame."* This shifts your attention to the immediate environment.
- **Safe Place Visualization:** Visualize a place where you feel safe and calm. Close your eyes and imagine a peaceful scene, such as a beach, a forest, or a cozy room. Focus on the details, like the sound of waves, the smell of pine trees, or the warmth of a blanket. This mental image can create a sense of safety and relaxation.
- **Positive Affirmations:** Repeat positive statements to yourself to reinforce a sense of control and safety. Say affirmations like *"I am safe right now,"* *"I can*

handle this," or *"I am in control."* These statements can help counteract negative thoughts and promote a sense of stability.

MOVEMENT BASED PRACTICES

Movement-based practices involve therapeutic approaches that use physical movement to help you process, manage, and heal from trauma. These practices identify the connection between the body and mind and use movement to release stored stress and tension from your mind. It also promotes emotional regulation and improves overall well-being.

The two most popular and effective movement-based practices include trauma-informed yoga and dance and movement therapy.

TRAUMA-INFORMED YOGA

Trauma-informed yoga is a mindfulness practice that encourages you to connect with yourself, feel your emotions without dissociating from your body, and avoid letting past experiences destroy your peace of mind. It is a specialized form of yoga designed to create a safe and supportive environment for individuals who have experienced trauma. It emphasizes mindfulness, body awareness, and the gentle release of tension.

The following are the key elements of this practice:

- The practice prioritizes creating a sense of safety and control. Instructors often offer options and encourage participants to choose what feels best for their bodies.
- It includes gentle, slow movements and restorative poses to avoid triggering stress responses and to promote relaxation.

- Trauma-informed yoga integrates mindfulness to help participants stay present and aware of their bodily sensations.
- Trauma-informed yoga involves controlled breathing exercises to help regulate the nervous system and reduce anxiety. Techniques such as diaphragmatic breathing or alternate nostril breathing can help participants manage stress and enhance relaxation.

DANCE AND MOVEMENT THERAPY (DMT)

Dance and movement therapy (DMT) is a psychotherapeutic use of movement to support emotional, cognitive, physical, and social integration. It leverages the expressive nature of movement to help individuals explore and process emotions and experiences. Studies show that DMT can significantly enhance body awareness and increase the feeling of safety and religious, spiritual, psychological, and cultural resources.[12]

Under this therapy, participants use spontaneous and expressive movements to explore and communicate their feelings and experiences. For instance, a therapist might encourage individuals to move in a way that expresses a specific emotion, such as joy, sadness, or anger, facilitating emotional release and insight.

CONTROLLED BREATHING EXERCISE

Controlled breathing, also known as counted breathing, is an effective technique for healing from the somatic effects of trauma. Controlled breathing exercises regulate breathing patterns to

---

[12] Impact of dance therapy on adults with psychological trauma: a systematic review - PMC (nih.gov)

promote physical and mental well-being. These exercises can significantly aid in managing stress, anxiety, and trauma-related symptoms by influencing the body's physiological responses.

Here is how controlled breathing exercises can promote healing:

Activation of the Parasympathetic Nervous System

The parasympathetic nervous system (PNS) controls the body's "rest and digest" functions. Controlled breathing activates the PNS, helping the body to relax and reduce stress.[13] Activation of the PNS slows down the heart rate and lowers blood pressure, promoting a sense of calm and relaxation. Moreover, controlled breathing exercises help decrease the production of stress hormones such as cortisol, aiding in relaxation and recovery from stress. Diaphragmatic breathing is an example of a controlled breathing exercise.

Reduction of Hyperventilation

Hyperventilation causes an imbalance between oxygen and carbon dioxide in the blood, leading to dizziness, lightheadedness, and increased anxiety. Controlled breathing helps restore this balance. By regulating breathing, controlled exercises can prevent or mitigate the onset of panic attacks, which are often triggered by hyperventilation. Breathing slowly and steadily reduces the likelihood of hyperventilation, promoting overall calmness. The pursed-lip breathing exercise can slow down the breathing rate and reduce hyperventilation.

---

[13] Use of controlled diaphragmatic breathing for the management of motion sickness in a virtual reality environment - PubMed (nih.gov)

Enhancement of Emotional Regulation

Controlled breathing fosters a stronger mind-body connection, helping individuals become more aware of their emotional states and bodily responses. Breathing exercises can help manage and regulate intense emotions such as anger, fear, and sadness. You can gain better control over their emotional responses by focusing on their breath. Regular practice of controlled breathing has been shown to reduce symptoms of anxiety and depression by promoting relaxation and emotional stability.

Controlled breathing exercises offer a powerful tool for managing stress, anxiety, and trauma-related symptoms. Integrating controlled breathing into daily practice can help individuals achieve a greater sense of calm, control, and resilience.

SPECIFIC BREATHING TECHNIQUES

Below are some effective controlled breathing techniques that can enhance your healing and help improve your outcomes.

Diaphragmatic Breathing

A breathing exercise engaging the diaphragm to improve breathing is known as diaphragmatic breathing. The diaphragm is an important muscle situated below your lungs and heart, which helps you breathe in and out. Besides facilitating breathing, the diaphragm also performs other essential bodily functions. Training your diaphragm to contract and expand your lungs improves breathing.

Here is how you can perform diaphragmatic breathing:

- Sit on a comfortable, flat surface, and relax your shoulders.
- Put one of your hands on your stomach and the other one on your chest.
- Breathe in through your nose while focusing on the air moving from your nostrils to your lungs.
- Exhale slowly through pursed lips, focusing on the air moving out of your mouth and your lungs contracting again.
- Repeat the process multiple times.

Box Breathing

Box breathing is a technique used to normalize breathing rhythms after a stressful experience. It is a simple yet effective technique to improve your breathing, relax your body, clear your mind, and improve your focus.

The following are the steps to perform box breathing:

- Sit comfortably, preferably on a chair, with your back supported by the chair and your feet touching the floor.
- Close your eyes and slowly breathe in through your nose for four seconds.
- Focus on the air entering your body through your nostrils and expanding your chest and stomach.
- Now, hold your breath while slowly counting to four. Try not to force your mouth shut while holding your breath.
- Slowly exhale while counting to four.
- Wait for four seconds before repeating the process two to three times.

4-7-8 BREATHING

The 4-7-8 breathing technique is a breathing exercise to help you improve your control over breathing. This technique is similar to the box breathing technique and helps improve your breathing, nerves, and sleep.

The steps for performing 4-7-8 breathing include the following:

- Sit in a comfortable position in a peaceful environment. You may lie down if you use this practice to fall asleep. Maintain a good posture.
- First, exhale through your mouth.
- Now, inhale through your nose while counting to four.
- Hold your breath for seven seconds.
- Now, exhale through your mouth for eight seconds. Make a whooshing sound while exhaling air.
- This completes one cycle of breath. Repeat the process for three to four cycles of breath initially. You can gradually increase it to seven to eight breath cycles.

Pursed-lip Breathing

Another simple yet effective technique is the pursed-lip breathing technique, which involves inhaling and exhaling. It helps treat shortness of breath by slowing your breathing pace.

To perform pursed-lip breathing, follow these steps:

- Sit in a comfortable position with your neck and shoulders in a relaxed posture.

- Place a hand on your stomach to feel the impact of inhaling and exhaling.
- Breathe in with your nose while keeping your mouth closed for two seconds. You do not need to take a deep breath.
- Now, purse your lips in a whistling or blowing position.
- Exhale slowly through your pursed lips while feeling your stomach shrinking gradually and returning to its original shape as you exhale completely.

Perform this exercise three to five times daily for 7-10 minutes each time. While performing this exercise, ensure you exhale longer than you inhale and avoid forcing air out of your lungs.

INTEGRATING MIND AND BODY THERAPIES

The compelling benefits of somatic experience therapy make it an effective treatment option for people dealing with trauma. However, while integrating mind-body therapies, you must keep the following factors in mind.

UNDERSTAND HOW TRAUMA IMPACTS YOU SPECIFICALLY

- Take time to reflect on how trauma has affected you personally, considering both physical and emotional symptoms.
- Recognize specific triggers that evoke distressing reactions or memories related to the trauma.
- Keep a journal to track your symptoms and how they fluctuate, helping you understand patterns and triggers.

BEGIN WITH TRAUMA-INFORMED YOGA

- Start with trauma-informed yoga, prioritizing safety, choice, and body awareness.
- Use yoga as a mindfulness practice to cultivate awareness of bodily sensations and emotions.
- Engage in gentle yoga poses and breathing exercises to release tension and promote relaxation.

INCORPORATE TAI CHI AND QIGONG

- Tai Chi and Qigong involve slow, flowing movements that promote relaxation and balance.
- These practices focus on balancing the body's energy flow (Qi) and promoting physical and emotional harmony.
- Incorporate Tai Chi and Qigong to enhance your mind-body connection and cultivate inner peace.

EXPLORE MEDITATION AND MINDFULNESS

- Practice meditation and mindfulness to develop present-moment awareness and non-judgmental acceptance.
- Use meditation to reduce stress, calm the mind, and regulate emotions.
- Incorporate mindfulness techniques such as deep breathing and body scanning to ground yourself during distress.

ENGAGE IN PROFESSIONAL SUPPORT

- Seek professional support from therapists or counselors trained in trauma-informed care.

- Participate in individual or group therapy sessions to explore and process traumatic experiences.
- Work with mind-body therapists who specialize in integrating physical and emotional healing modalities.

PRACTICE SELF-CARE AND PATIENCE

- Practice self-care and self-compassion, acknowledging your strengths and limitations.
- Set achievable goals for your healing journey, and be patient with yourself as you progress.
- Engage in activities that bring you joy and relaxation, such as spending time in nature, creative expression, or connecting with loved ones.

GRADUAL EXPOSURE TO DRIVING

- Gradually expose yourself to driving situations, starting with less challenging scenarios and progressively increasing difficulty.
- Use mindfulness and relaxation techniques while driving to stay grounded and manage your anxiety.
- Consider seeking support from a driving instructor or therapist specializing in anxiety management.

These considerations ensure the smooth integration of key body-mind techniques in your life.

SUMMARY BOX: SOMATIC EXPERIENCING (SE) TECHNIQUES

Somatic experiencing is a body-mind technique focused on healing trauma by shifting the focus. It involves encouraging the trauma survivors to focus on their bodies rather than stressful thoughts to enhance their treatment and recovery. Below is a quick overview of key somatic experience techniques.

Building Body Awareness: Develop a keen awareness of bodily sensations, movements, and physiological responses, allowing for a deeper understanding of how trauma manifests in the body.

Resourcing: Identify and cultivate internal and external resources that provide a sense of safety, stability, and support. These resources can include positive memories, strengths, supportive relationships, grounding techniques, and relaxation exercises.

Pendulation: Practice shifting attention between distressing sensations or emotions and feelings of safety and calmness. It helps prevent overwhelm and facilitates the gradual processing and integration of traumatic material.

Titration: Approach traumatic memories or sensations in small, manageable doses, allowing for gentle and gradual processing. By breaking down overwhelming experiences into smaller components, individuals can safely explore and release traumatic material without becoming re-traumatized.

Grounding Techniques: Utilize grounding techniques to stay connected to the present moment and regulate arousal levels. These techniques help you feel more stable and grounded, reducing the intensity of trauma-related symptoms.

Movement and Physical Discharge: Engage in physical movement and expression to release stored tension and trauma from the body. Activities such as yoga, dance, tai chi, or expressive arts allow you to discharge excess energy, process emotional experiences, and reconnect with your body.

Integration: Integrate fragmented aspects of traumatic experiences into a coherent narrative, fostering healing and resilience. This process involves making meaning of the trauma, finding a sense of closure, and incorporating the experience into one's identity.

CONCLUSION

Healing from trauma may seem easier said than done; however, it does not have to be overwhelming. Trauma can have profound effects on both the mind and body, impacting you in unique ways. Integrating mind and body therapies can be an effective approach to healing from trauma and promoting overall well-being. It ensures a holistic treatment and recovery approach with adequate focus on body and mind.

Once you take the necessary steps to identify and treat the somatic symptoms of a traumatic experience, you can proceed to the next step in recovery, which involves getting back on the road and regaining your confidence. Adopting a holistic approach toward trauma healing techniques will enable you to gradually rebuild the confidence to drive again, focusing on creating a sense of safety and control to drive with confidence again.

Chapter Four

REBUILDING SAFETY AND TRUST IN DRIVING

"The only thing that stands between you and your dream is the will to try and the belief that it is actually possible."

—Joel Brown

Building confidence while driving takes moderate, methodical stages rather than one big leap. Whether you are learning to drive for the first time or seeking to rebuild your confidence after a traumatic crash, the key lies in gradual and consistent efforts.

Rebuilding trust in your driving ability after a traumatic incident is a gradual process. It doesn't happen overnight, nor is it a journey that can be rushed. Like learning to walk again after a physical injury, regaining confidence behind the wheel requires patience, persistence, and small, intentional actions. Each step forward, no matter how minor it may seem, is a significant achievement toward reclaiming your sense of control and normalcy.

By now, you should be well on your way to recuperating from

your terrible experience. Now it is time for the step that might have been a nightmare for you after the crash—getting back on the road.

CREATING A SAFE DRIVING ENVIRONMENT

First things first, before getting back on the roads, it is crucial to create a safe driving environment for yourself. It involves the following aspects:

PSYCHOLOGICAL AND EMOTIONAL SAFETY

Building trust in driving goes beyond physical safety; it also involves creating a psychologically and emotionally supportive environment. Here is how you can achieve that:

Develop and Maintain a Routine and Structure

Begin by gaining control of your routine by developing and sticking to a schedule. A schedule instills a sense of normalcy and control and motivates you to take charge of the wheel again. Create a regular schedule for driving. Start with short, predictable trips at the same time each day. This routine can help reduce anxiety by making the experience more familiar and less daunting. Moreover, break down your driving recovery into manageable steps. Set small, achievable goals, such as driving around the block, then gradually increase to more challenging routes. Celebrate each milestone to build confidence.

When creating a routine, try to initially stick to routes you are comfortable with. Familiarity can provide a sense of security and help reduce stress. As you build confidence, you can gradually introduce new routes and more complex driving situations.

Commit to the Mindfulness Strategies

Leverage the solutions and strategies discussed in the previous chapters to help develop the resilience and strength you need on your journey. Consider seeking professional help for better outcomes. Regularly attend sessions with a therapist or counselor who specializes in trauma recovery. Professional guidance can provide tailored strategies to manage your fear and anxiety, helping you stay on track with your recovery.

Incorporate mindfulness and meditation practices into your daily routine. These techniques can help you stay calm and focused on and off the road. Set aside specific times each day for mindfulness exercises to reduce overall anxiety.

Actively engage with your support network, including family, friends, and support groups. Regular communication and shared experiences can provide emotional reassurance and practical advice. Lean on your support system during challenging times to reinforce your sense of security.

PHYSICAL SAFETY

Ensure your physical safety by gradually exposing yourself to driving on the roads again. Begin with short drives on familiar roads. This reduces the unpredictability of the environment and allows you to build confidence in a controlled setting. Gradually increase the duration and complexity of your drives. Move from quiet residential streets to more trafficked roads at a pace that feels manageable for you.

An effective strategy is to use empty parking lots or other controlled environments to practice driving. This can help you rebuild your basic driving skills without the pressure of traffic. Moreover, consider using driving simulators that can mimic real-world driving conditions. This can provide a safe way to practice and build confidence without the risks of actual road driving.

Follow Safe Driving Practices

Make sure you know and understand safe driving practices and strategies to enhance your safety. Keep your attention on driving by minimizing in-car distractions. Avoid using your phone, eating, or engaging in other activities that can take your focus away from the road.

If necessary, use hands-free devices and car features that enhance safety, such as backup cameras and lane-keeping assist systems.

Maintain Your Focus

Use mindfulness techniques while driving to stay present and focused. Techniques such as deep breathing and staying aware of your surroundings can help keep your mind on the task at hand. Take regular breaks during longer drives to rest and refresh your mind. This can prevent fatigue and help you maintain focus over extended periods.

Make a Safe Driving Plan

Create a pre-drive checklist to ensure your vehicle is in good condition. Check tire pressure fluid levels and ensure that all lights and signals are working properly. Plan your routes in advance to avoid high-stress driving situations. Use GPS to find the safest and least congested routes to your destination.

Keep an emergency kit in your car, including items such as a first-aid kit, a flashlight, a blanket, and basic tools. Knowing you are prepared for emergencies can provide peace of mind.

VEHICLE SAFETY

Ensuring your vehicle is in optimal condition is crucial for safe driving. Regular maintenance and checks can prevent unexpected breakdowns and reduce anxiety about mechanical issues.

Tire Pressure: Check your tire pressure regularly, ideally once a month and before long trips. Properly inflated tires improve fuel efficiency and handling and reduce the risk of blowouts. Refer to your vehicle's manual or the sticker inside the driver's door for the recommended tire pressure. Use a reliable tire gauge to check and adjust the pressure as needed.

Brakes and Braking System: Have your brakes inspected at least once a year. Pay attention to any signs of wear, such as squealing, grinding noises, or a spongy brake pedal. Check the brake fluid regularly and ensure it is at the proper level. Low brake fluid can affect braking performance.

Wheel Alignment and Balancing: Get your wheel alignment checked annually or whenever you notice uneven tire wear or the vehicle pulling to one side. Proper alignment ensures better handling and extends tire life. Ensure your tires are balanced correctly to avoid vibrations, especially at higher speeds. Unbalanced tires can lead to uneven wear and tear.

Lights: Regularly check all vehicle lights, including headlights, taillights, brake lights, and turn signals. Ensure they are functioning correctly, and replace any burned-out bulbs promptly. Clean your light lenses to ensure maximum visibility. Cloudy or dirty lenses can reduce the effectiveness of your lights.

Steering: Ensure your steering system operates smoothly. If you notice any difficulty in steering or unusual noises, have it inspected by a professional. Check the power steering fluid level regularly. Low fluid can make steering more difficult and damage the power steering pump.

Fluids: Regularly check all vehicle fluids, including engine oil, coolant, transmission fluid, and windshield washer fluid. Keeping these fluids at optimal levels ensures your vehicle runs smoothly. Follow your vehicle's maintenance schedule for fluid changes. Regular oil changes and coolant flushes can prevent engine problems.

ENVIRONMENTAL AND PERSONAL ADJUSTMENTS

After ensuring physical safety measures, you must make adjustments to ensure your safety and comfort within and outside the vehicle.

Adjust your Vehicle Settings for Comfort

When it comes to safe driving, prioritize comfort. Make sure your vehicle settings are adjusted to your preferences and comfort. You can take the following steps to adjust your vehicle settings for enhanced comfort:

- **Seat Position:** Adjust your seat to ensure you have a clear view of the road and your mirrors. Your seat should be positioned so that you can comfortably reach all the pedals and controls without straining. Ensure your headrest is properly positioned to protect your neck in case of a collision.
- **Mirrors:** Adjust your side and rearview mirrors to eliminate blind spots. A well-positioned mirror setup can significantly enhance your awareness of the surrounding traffic. Regularly clean your mirrors to maintain clear visibility.
- **Climate Control:** Set your car's climate control to a comfortable temperature to prevent discomfort and distraction. Proper ventilation can also reduce fatigue during long drives.
- **Steering Wheel:** Adjust the steering wheel so that you can comfortably hold it without stretching or slouching. Your arms should be slightly bent when holding the wheel at the 9 and 3 o'clock positions.

Plan your Routes

Always begin by driving on familiar routes to build your confidence, and then proceed to unfamiliar routes. Make sure you plan your routes to avoid any uncertain situations or inconveniences. For better route planning, you can use navigation tools such as GPS or smartphone applications to plan your route ahead of time. Early planning helps with mental preparation and saves you from the undue stress that comes with driving on unfamiliar routes.

Another important task on your checklist must be to check the weather forecast and traffic updates. Try to avoid congested areas to reduce the risk of crashes. Although it is better to drive on familiar routes, if you are driving to a new destination, try to learn about the route beforehand and note any potential hazards or challenging intersections. When going on longer drives, plan for rest stops to provide yourself with some time to freshen up and prevent fatigue.

If possible, avoid driving in areas known for high-traffic crashes or poor road conditions. Choose routes with better lighting and road quality. These practices significantly enhance your safety and minimize the potential risk of accidents or any other uncertain situations.

Adopt a Mentality of Emergency Preparedness

An emergency can happen to anyone at any time. As an adept driver, you must be prepared for it in advance. It not only involves having emergency tools and equipment but also being mentally prepared for any uncertain situation that you may face. Adopting a mentality of emergency preparedness not only ensures your safety but also the safety of others and the environment.

Stress and anxiety can impair your ability to react appropriately to sudden changes on the road. Practice keeping a composed mindset during your drives, and try to handle even uncertain situations with calmness. Always keep an emergency kit in your car, including items such as a first-aid kit, flashlight, blankets, water, and non-perishable snacks. This can be crucial in the event of a breakdown or crash. It is also good to have a power bank or a car charger available to charge your phone during emergencies.

Moreover, you must be familiar with basic emergency procedures such as changing a tire, using jumper cables, and handling minor car repairs. These repairs can help you fix several issues on your own and help yourself and others in emergencies. Ensure that your car has safety features such as hazard lights and emergency brakes, and practice using them to be able to use them proficiently when the need arises.

STEPS TO REGAIN DRIVING CONFIDENCE

The first drive after a traumatic experience is a significant step forward in your healing. Besides polishing your driving skills, it is crucial to regain your confidence, which might have been lost due to the unpleasant experience.

Start Small

Regaining driving confidence begins with taking manageable steps. Start by driving short distances in familiar areas during times when traffic is light. This approach allows you to reacquaint yourself with the act of driving in a low-pressure environment. Familiar routes provide a sense of security and control, reducing anxiety and allowing you to focus on gradually building your confidence.

Be Consistent

Integrating the relaxation techniques you have learned previously into your driving routine is essential for making worthwhile progress. Whether it is deep breathing exercises, mindfulness practices, or visualization strategies, these techniques can help manage anxiety and keep you calm behind the wheel. Consistency is key; the more you practice these techniques, the more they become second nature, helping to ease your nerves before and during your drives.

Take a Defensive Driving Course

Consider enrolling in a defensive driving course. These courses are designed to improve your driving skills and teach you how to anticipate and respond to potential hazards on the road. Equipping yourself with these skills can make you feel more prepared and confident when encountering various driving situations. Defensive driving courses also often include practical sessions, allowing you to apply what you have learned in a controlled setting.

Drive with a Companion

Having a trusted companion accompany you in the vehicle you are driving can be a source of support and reassurance, especially when trying to get back on the road after a traumatic experience. Whether it is a family member, relative, friend, or even a driving instructor, the presence of a trusted individual can help reduce anxiety. They can also provide you with immediate assistance if needed, as well as words of encouragement and constructive feedback to help you improve your performance.

Gradually Increase Driving Challenges

Initially, it might seem difficult to drive again; however, as you take small steps, your confidence grows, and things begin getting easier. As your confidence increases, the complexity of your driving gradually increases, including driving long distances or facing more traffic. This gradual increase in the driving challenges helps build your confidence and resilience and overcome your fears without overwhelming you.

Celebrate Small Wins

Monitoring your progress and acknowledging the achievement of every milestone is an effective strategy to boost your confidence and improve your driving skills. Even if some wins seem smaller, do not forget to acknowledge them and appreciate yourself for achieving them. From driving to a new location to handling a different traffic situation without feeling anxious, every little step contributes to the overall outcome of your journey. Make your wins a source of motivation to keep pushing forward towards your goal attainment.

Be Patient with Yourself

Recovery and rebuilding confidence are processes that take time. It is important to be patient and kind to yourself throughout this journey. Understand that setbacks are a natural part of the process, and they do not negate the progress you have made. Give yourself permission to move at your own pace and acknowledge the effort you are putting into overcoming your fears.

By following these steps, you can gradually rebuild your driving confidence. Each step is designed to create a sense of safety and control, empowering you to reclaim your ability to drive without fear or anxiety.

Tools and Support for Safe Driving

Incorporating technology into your recovery measures can significantly enhance your overall outcomes and help you return to the road better and more confidently. Leverage the following technologies into your driving routine to stay focused, reduce anxiety, and reinforce the safe driving practices you are developing.

SAFE DRIVING APPS AND TOOLS

When it comes to technological aids for safe driving, several apps and tools are designed to enhance driving safety. These tools can provide valuable support as you work to rebuild your confidence and ensure a safer driving experience.

OnMyWay

OnMyWay is a unique app that incentivizes safe driving by rewarding users for not using their phones while driving. For every mile driven without texting or using the phone, users earn rewards that can be redeemed for various discounts and offers. This not only promotes safer driving habits but also provides a tangible benefit for staying focused on the road.

SAFE 2 SAVE

SAFE 2 SAVE is another app that rewards drivers for putting their phones away while driving. Users earn points for every minute of distraction-free driving, which can then be redeemed at participating businesses. This app helps to encourage and maintain safe driving practices, making the roads safer for everyone.

TrueMotion Family Safe Driving

TrueMotion Family Safe Driving is an app designed to keep families connected and safe on the road. It tracks driving habits and provides feedback on how to improve. The app also offers location sharing so family members can see where their loved ones are in real time, adding an extra layer of security and peace of mind.

I'm Driving

I'm Driving is a simple app that sends automatic replies to incoming texts and calls, informing the sender that you are driving and will get back to them later. This helps to reduce distractions and allows you to focus fully on the road. By minimizing interruptions, you can drive more safely and confidently.

These apps and tools can be integral to creating a safer driving environment. They not only promote good driving habits but also provide reassurance and support as you work to regain your confidence behind the wheel.

DEFENSIVE DRIVING AND SAFETY PRINCIPLES

Defensive driving refers to the driving approach involving the anticipation of potential hazards and dangerous situations based on the analysis of factors and circumstances. This anticipation allows you to adopt a driving approach based on personal and environmental safety. In order to ensure a safe driving experience, adopt defensive driving techniques, such as maintaining a safe following distance, being aware of your surroundings, and anticipating other drivers' actions. You must always use seat belts and ensure all passengers are buckled up before driving.

Defensive Driving Course

Enrolling in a defensive driving course can be an excellent step toward rebuilding your confidence on the road. These courses teach practical techniques to help you anticipate and respond to potential hazards, ultimately making you a safer and more confident driver.

Here are some examples of what you might learn in a defensive driving course:

- Understanding and applying safe following distances to allow enough time to react to sudden stops.
- Techniques for managing and avoiding distractions, such as setting your GPS and playlist before you start driving.
- Strategies for handling difficult driving conditions, like inclement weather or heavy traffic.

Taking a defensive driving course not only refreshes your driving skills but also instills a sense of preparedness and control, which is crucial for regaining confidence.

LLLC Principle

One fundamental aspect of defensive driving is the LLLC Principle, which stands for Look ahead, Look around, Leave room, and Communicate. This principle provides a framework for maintaining awareness and safety on the road.

The following are the key elements of the LLLC principle:

- **Look Ahead:** Always scan the road ahead to anticipate potential problems. This means not just looking at the car directly in front of you but also keeping an eye on the overall traffic flow and any upcoming hazards.
- **Look Around:** Use your mirrors frequently and be aware of your surroundings. This includes checking your blind spots before changing lanes and being mindful of pedestrians, cyclists, and other vehicles.

- **Leave Room:** Maintain a safe distance from the vehicle in front of you to allow for sudden stops. Also, ensure you have enough space on all sides of your vehicle, especially when driving at higher speeds or in heavy traffic.
- **Communicate:** Use your signals, horns, and lights to communicate your intentions to other drivers. Clear communication can help prevent misunderstandings and accidents.

Vehicle Maintenance and Inspection

Ensuring your vehicle is in good working condition is another critical aspect of safe driving. Regular maintenance and inspections can prevent breakdowns and accidents caused by mechanical failures. Here are some key areas to focus on:

- **Tire Pressure:** Check your tire pressure regularly to ensure proper inflation, which affects handling, fuel efficiency, and tire lifespan.
- **Brakes and Braking System:** Regularly inspect your brakes for wear and tear. Ensure your brake pads, rotors, and fluid are in good condition to maintain optimal braking performance.
- **Wheel Alignment and Balancing:** Proper alignment and balancing of your wheels ensure even tire wear and improve handling.
- **Lights:** Regularly check all your lights, including headlights, brake lights, and turn signals, to ensure they are functioning correctly. This is crucial for visibility and communication with other drivers.
- **Steering:** Inspect your steering system for any issues, such as unusual noises or difficulty turning the wheel, which could indicate problems.

- **Fluids:** Regularly check and top up all essential fluids, including engine oil, coolant, brake fluid, and transmission fluid, to keep your vehicle running smoothly.
- **Built-in Safety Features:** Familiarize yourself with your car's built-in safety features, such as anti-lock brakes (ABS), traction control, and airbags, and ensure they are functioning properly.

These steps help build a sense of security and control, which is essential for regaining your confidence on the road.

LEGAL AND REGULATORY SUPPORT

Besides implementing other measures, legal and regulatory support is also crucial to building your confidence.

Consider taking the following steps:

Road Safety Laws

Before taking your vehicle on the road, you must familiarize yourself with road safety rules and laws. This knowledge is crucial for creating a safe driving environment and rebuilding your confidence after a traumatic experience. These laws are designed to protect all road users and ensure a systematic flow of traffic. Here are some key areas to focus on:

- **Speed Limits:** Always observe and adhere to the posted speed limits. Speed limits are set based on road conditions, traffic patterns, and safety considerations.

- **Seat Belt Laws:** Wearing a seat belt is mandatory in most regions. It significantly reduces the risk of injury or death in the event of an accident.
- **Distracted Driving Laws:** Many areas have laws prohibiting the use of handheld devices while driving. Avoid using your phone or other distractions to maintain focus on the road.
- **DUI Regulations:** Driving under the influence of alcohol or drugs is illegal and extremely dangerous. Be aware of the legal limits and ensure you are sober before getting behind the wheel.
- **Traffic Signals and Signs:** Obey all traffic signals and signs. These are in place to regulate traffic flow and ensure safety at intersections, pedestrian crossings, and other critical areas.

Driver Assistance Technologies

Modern vehicles are equipped with various driver assistance technologies designed to enhance safety and make driving easier and safer.

Getting to know these modern, innovative technologies can provide you with more confidence and help when driving.

- **Anti-lock Braking System (ABS):** Prevents the wheels from locking up during braking, allowing you to maintain steering control. This is particularly useful in slippery conditions.
- **Electronic Stability Control (ESC):** Helps maintain control of the vehicle during extreme steering maneuvers by reducing the risk of skidding or losing control.

- **Adaptive Cruise Control (ACC):** Automatically adjust your speed to maintain a safe distance from the vehicle ahead. This is useful for highway driving and reduces the need for constant speed adjustments.
- **Lane Departure Warning (LDW):** This alerts you if the vehicle begins to drift out of its lane unintentionally. This helps prevent accidents caused by distracted or drowsy driving.
- **Blind Spot Detection (BSD):** Monitors the areas around your vehicle that are not visible in your mirrors and alerts you if there is another vehicle in your blind spot.
- **Forward Collision Warning (FCW) and Automatic Emergency Braking (AEB):** FCW alerts you to a potential front-end collision, while AEB can automatically apply the brakes if a collision is imminent and you do not react in time.

By understanding and utilizing these legal and technological supports, you can enhance your driving safety and confidence. These measures not only help prevent crashes but also provide peace of mind, knowing that you are taking all necessary steps to protect yourself and others on the road. This foundation of safety and support is critical as you continue to rebuild trust in your driving abilities.

CHECKLIST/STEP-BY-STEP GUIDE/ SUMMARY OF HOW TO REGAIN TRUST BEHIND THE WHEEL

- Step 1: Address the emotional impact
- Step 2: Reacquaint yourself with driving

- Step 3: Gradual exposure
- Step 4: Defensive driving skills
- Step 5: Build positive experiences
- Step 6: Visit the accident site
- Step 7: Enhance vehicle safety
- Step 8: Psychological techniques (as discussed in previous chapters)
- Step 9: Review insurance and legal matters *(This will provide you with a sense of closure, which will reduce lingering stress associated with the accident)*
- Step 10: Be patient and persistent

BEST TIPS FOR DRIVING SAFELY IN ADVERSE WEATHER CONDITIONS

- Drive slowly
- Increase following distance
- Use appropriate lights
- Avoid unnecessary lane changes
- Prepare your vehicle
- Avoid driving through flooded areas
- Be cautious of aquaplaning
- Plan ahead
- Keep emergency supplies
- Stay alert

Make these practices a part of your driving routine to ensure a safe driving experience.

CONCLUSION

Rebuilding safety and trust in driving is a seemingly challenging yet crucial task that you must undertake in order to systematically approach your recovery. I know that getting back on the road after a traumatic crash is more challenging than it might seem. The psychological impacts and the flashbacks never leave your side and tend to intensify as soon as you try to drive again. However, your fears are only terrifying as long as you do not take any proactive steps towards dealing with them. Once you take the initial steps to recovery, things gradually begin improving as you go along the way. Getting back on the road and gradually building your confidence completes the second step of the SAFE recovery framework. It prepares you for the third step, which involves leveraging the confidence gained through your consistent driving practice and building and utilizing a strong support system to maintain that confidence while you return to driving with a safer approach.

Part Three

FORTIFY YOUR SUPPORT SYSTEM

Chapter Five

SUPPORT NETWORKS AND THEIR ROLE IN YOUR RECOVERY

"I am building a healthy support system and learning to use it readily."

—**Maureen Brady**

Recovery does not happen in isolation. It is a communal journey. However, many trauma survivors resort to solitude and avoid social interaction post-crash. Various studies highlight that traumatic experiences often lead to a tendency to avoid social interaction.[14] The road to recovery is often misunderstood as a solitary path—one where we muster all our strength and courage to overcome our struggles alone.

The truth is that healing, especially from trauma, is rarely achieved in isolation. It is a collective effort that thrives on the support, encouragement, and understanding of those around us.

Regardless of how tempting it might feel to cut yourself off

---

[14] Social interaction in the aftermath of conflict-related trauma experiences among women in Walungu Territory, Democratic Republic of Congo - PMC (nih.gov)

from others and find peace in a cozy corner of your home, the real strength lies in facing your fears and leveraging the support from those around you to deal with them. In the aftermath of a traumatic road accident, the importance of a robust support network cannot be overstated. Friends, family, healthcare professionals, and community groups all play pivotal roles in your journey toward recovery. This is what the third step of our SAFE road recovery framework entails—establishing and leveraging a robust support network for trauma healing and recovery.

ROLE OF A SUPPORT NETWORK IN RECOVERY

Being involved in a car crash, whether as a driver, passenger, or witness, is a traumatic experience that can disrupt your life in significant ways. However, through the right recovery measures, you can minimize that disruption in your life and return to normalcy soon. One of those measures is building and leveraging a support network, as it can facilitate your recovery in the following ways:

EMOTIONAL SUPPORT

After a traumatic car crash, it is common to feel isolated and misunderstood. Support networks, including family, friends, and community groups, help bridge this gap by offering a sense of belonging and shared experience. The support and involvement of supportive individuals in your life help reduce the isolating effects of trauma. It also fosters a more positive and connected outlook during recovery.

Providing a safe space for expressing emotions and processing the traumatic event

Talking about the traumatic event is a vital part of healing, but it is often difficult to do so. A trusted support network provides a safe space where you can openly express your feelings without judgment. This emotional outlet is crucial for processing the trauma, as it allows you to confront and work through your emotions rather than suppressing them. Being able to articulate your experience helps you understand and integrate the event into your broader life narrative.

Offering comfort and understanding from family and friends

Family and friends offer a unique form of comfort and understanding that professional relationships may lack. Their personal connection to you means they can provide support tailored to your specific needs and personality. Their presence can be a source of immense reassurance and stability, reminding you that you are not alone in your journey. The empathy and care from loved ones can provide immediate relief and long-term emotional sustenance, helping you navigate the complex emotions that follow a traumatic accident.

PROFESSIONAL SUPPORT

In the aftermath of a traumatic car crash, professional support becomes an invaluable component of the recovery process. This support typically involves assistance from healthcare providers, legal advisors, and workplace accommodations. It also involves the diagnosis and treatment of physical and psychological injuries from the accident.

Legal advisors help you fulfill the legal formalities, ensuring that your rights are protected and that you understand the process of seeking compensation. Additionally, workplace accommodations may be necessary to help you return to work safely and effectively, considering any physical or psychological limitations.

Diagnosis and treatment of physical and psychological injuries from the accident

Healthcare providers are essential in identifying and treating both the visible and invisible injuries sustained in a crash. Immediate medical attention can address physical injuries such as fractures, sprains, and whiplash.

Psychological injuries, such as post-traumatic stress disorder (PTSD), anxiety, and depression, often require specialized care from mental health professionals. Early and accurate diagnosis of these conditions is critical for effective treatment and recovery.

Understanding your legal rights (including how to seek compensation)

Car crashes often bring about a host of legal issues, from insurance claims to potential lawsuits. Legal advisors help you understand your rights and the best course of action to seek compensation for damages. This includes navigating the claims process, collecting and presenting evidence, and negotiating settlements. Understanding your legal rights ensures that you receive the compensation necessary to cover medical expenses, lost wages, and other associated costs.

Legal support also provides peace of mind, allowing you to focus more fully on your recovery without the added stress of legal uncertainties.

PRACTICAL SUPPORT

Practical support is essential in the recovery journey after a traumatic car crash, providing assistance with daily tasks and responsibilities that may have become challenging. This support can come from personal networks and professional services, ensuring a holistic approach to managing the incident's aftermath.

Following a crash, even routine activities can become overwhelming or physically impossible. Practical support from family, friends, and community members can significantly ease this burden. This might include assisting with household chores, running errands, transportation, child care, and appointments. Having a support system, including professional services such as physical therapy, to handle these tasks allows you to focus on recovery without the added stress of maintaining everyday responsibilities.

By combining help from personal support networks with professional services, practical support creates a comprehensive safety net for your healing and recovery.

IDENTIFYING YOUR SUPPORT NETWORK

Building a support network is not enough if the individuals in your support network are not the right fit for you. They may be supportive, knowledgeable, and kind, but they would not really support you if they do not align with your goals and needs. The first step to building a strong support network is identifying the individuals who can be a part of your network.

The following are the ways to identify your support network:

IDENTIFY YOUR NEEDS

Just like every trauma experience is different, the recovery needs also vary among survivors. Therefore, it is crucial to identify your unique needs and communicate them clearly to understand what kind of people you want to connect with. Reflect on your emotional, physical, and practical requirements. If you are looking for emotional support, professional advice, or help with daily tasks, clarifying your needs will guide you in finding a group that meets your expectations.

ASK FOR RECOMMENDATIONS

Another way to find viable resources is through recommendations. Reach out to healthcare providers, therapists, and trusted individuals in your community for recommendations. They often have insights into reputable support groups that can cater to your specific needs. Similarly, friends or family members who have been through similar experiences might also have valuable suggestions.

DO YOUR RESEARCH

Look into various support groups online or through community resources. Websites like Home Health Companions, Mayo Clinic, and Here to Help BC offer valuable information on finding and choosing the right support group. Pay attention to groups' missions, goals, and member testimonials to gauge their suitability.

ATTEND MEETINGS

Participate in a few meetings of potential support groups before committing. This firsthand experience will help you understand the group's dynamics, the topics discussed, and the support offered. It also allows you to interact with members and see if their experiences and outlook align with yours.

BE OPEN-MINDED

When exploring different support groups, keep an open mind. Each group has its own approach and atmosphere; you might find value in unexpected places. Being open to various types of support can broaden your options and increase your chances of finding a good fit.

CONSIDER THE FORMAT

Support groups can vary in format, including in-person meetings, online forums, and hybrid models. Consider the best format for you based on your comfort level, schedule, and accessibility. Online groups might offer more flexibility, while in-person meetings can provide a sense of community.

EVALUATE THE GROUP'S STRUCTURE

Assess the structure of the support group, including how meetings are conducted, the rules and guidelines in place, and the frequency of meetings. A well-organized group with clear guidelines can provide a stable and supportive environment.

ASSESS THE FACILITATOR

The facilitator plays a critical role in guiding discussions and maintaining a supportive atmosphere. Evaluate the facilitator's qualifications, experience, and approach. A skilled facilitator can help ensure that meetings are productive and that all members feel heard and supported.

CHECK AFFILIATIONS

Some support groups are affiliated with larger organizations or healthcare providers. These affiliations can lend credibility and provide additional resources. Check if the group is connected to reputable institutions, which can enhance the support offered.

TRUST YOUR INSTINCTS

Ultimately, it all comes down to your gut feelings. Trust your instincts when choosing a support group. If you feel comfortable, supported, and understood in a particular group, it is likely the right fit for you. Your gut feeling can be a reliable indicator of whether a group will meet your needs and contribute positively to your recovery.

By following these steps, you can find a support group that aligns with your needs and provides the essential support to aid your recovery from a traumatic car accident.

WHERE TO FIND THE RIGHT SUPPORT GROUPS

Once you know the steps to building your support network, the next step is to look for the right places to find those groups. The following are some sources where you can connect with the right individuals to be a part of your support group.

Note: A comprehensive list of resources, including specific resources for each of these categories, is presented toward the end of this chapter.

ONLINE PLATFORMS AND WEBSITES

Online platforms are convenient for finding support groups that fit your schedule and preferences. Various websites host virtual support groups where you can connect with others who share similar experiences and challenges. These platforms offer forums, chat rooms, and video conferencing options to facilitate communication and support.

LOCAL HOSPITALS AND REHABILITATION CENTERS

Hospitals and rehabilitation centers often provide support groups as part of their patient care services. These groups are usually facilitated by healthcare professionals and can offer a structured environment for recovery. Contacting your local hospital or rehab center can provide you with information on available support groups and meeting times.

NATIONAL AND LOCAL NON-PROFITS

Non-profit organizations at both national and local levels often organize support groups for individuals dealing with trauma and recovery. These organizations may offer in-person and virtual group meetings and additional resources such as educational materials and counseling services. Reaching out to non-profits dedicated to mental health and trauma recovery can lead you to supportive communities.

SOCIAL MEDIA PLATFORMS

Social media platforms can be a valuable resource for finding support groups. Groups on platforms like Facebook and Instagram allow you to connect with others in similar situations, share experiences, and receive support. Many of these groups are private, ensuring a safe space for members to discuss their challenges and progress.

SPECIALIZED SUPPORT SERVICES

Certain services are tailored to specific populations, such as veterans, survivors of specific types of trauma, or those affected by drunk driving crashes. These specialized support services often provide targeted resources and support groups that address the unique needs of their members.

CONSULTING WITH PROFESSIONALS

Healthcare and legal professionals can be excellent sources for finding support groups. Therapists, counselors, and primary care physicians often have lists of recommended groups and can provide referrals based on your specific needs. Legal advisors can also suggest support groups that offer assistance with navigating the aftermath of car crashes and dealing with legal issues.

By exploring these resources, you can find a support group that offers the emotional, practical, and professional assistance necessary for your recovery. Each type of resource provides different benefits, and by considering your specific needs and preferences, you can find a group that best supports your journey to healing.

WAYS TO ENGAGE FAMILY AND FRIENDS IN YOUR RECOVERY

Various studies highlight the significance of social support obtained through friends, family, and community for effective recovery.[15] You can make your loved ones a part of your recovery in the following ways:

EXPRESS YOUR NEEDS

Communication is key when it comes to emotional support. Clearly expressing your needs to family and friends helps them understand how they can assist you best. Whether you need someone to listen, offer words of encouragement, or provide a sense of normalcy, being open about your feelings and requirements can foster a supportive environment.

PARTICIPATE IN SUPPORT GROUPS TOGETHER

Attending support groups with a family member or friend can provide additional comfort and solidarity. Having a familiar face alongside you can ease the anxiety of joining a new group and reinforce the sense of a shared journey. It also helps your loved ones understand the challenges you face and how they can support you more effectively.

---

[15] The Role of Social Support in Coping with Psychological Trauma: An Integrated Biopsychosocial Model for Posttraumatic Stress Recovery - PMC (nih.gov)

SHARE EDUCATIONAL RESOURCES

Providing your family and friends with educational resources about trauma and recovery can help them comprehend what you're going through. Sharing articles, books, or videos on the psychological impacts of car crashes and effective coping strategies equips them with the knowledge to offer better support. It also opens up avenues for meaningful discussions about your experiences and needs.

COMMUNICATE CLEARLY

Maintain an open and uninterrupted communication channel with your support group. Clear communication builds the foundation for long-term relationships. Make sure your communication involves the following key elements:

- **Open Dialogue:** Have an open dialogue with your support group where you can share your problems, needs, goals, and expectations without any hindrance. This dialogue must be mutual and allow all parties to share their ideas and feedback to promote a healthy discussion and efficient outcome.
- **Set Expectations:** Do not expect others to understand what you want without explaining it to them clearly. Unclear expectations lead to confusion and failure to attain goals. Contrarily, clear expectations facilitate the timely fulfillment of your desired goals.
- **Use "I" Statements:** When seeking help from your network, adopt a direct approach, and rather than using indirect statements, opt for I statements. For instance, instead

of "Can you help me?" ask, "I need your help dealing with this task." This assertiveness can have a significant impact on your overall goal accomplishment.

Communication plays a key role in helping you build a strong network. It is also instrumental in allowing you to leverage that network in an efficient and effective manner.

DELEGATE TASKS

Do not hesitate to delegate tasks to family and friends. Your relationship with them must be based on confidence and mutual trust rather than hesitation. Identify areas where you need assistance, such as household chores, grocery shopping, or appointments. Clear delegation ensures that responsibilities are shared and you are not overburdened.

PLAN TOGETHER

Planning tasks and activities together can make the process more manageable and less stressful. Sit down with your loved ones and create a schedule or to-do list. Collaborative planning helps ensure that everyone is aware of their roles and responsibilities, promoting a sense of teamwork and cooperation.

By implementing these communication strategies and practical help approaches, you can effectively engage your family and friends in your recovery journey. Their support, combined with your openness and clear communication, creates a robust network that can significantly enhance your healing process.

USE OF PROFESSIONAL AND COMMUNITY RESOURCES

Effective recovery begins with the efficient discovery and utilization of available professional and community resources. Many trauma survivors often overlook the wealth of resources available to them and fail to realize their potential in their healing. From medical assistance to legal help, you can find some of the best resources within your community to facilitate your recovery.

The following are the key areas in which you must utilize these resources:

MEDICAL ATTENTION

Seeking immediate medical attention after a car crash is vital, even if injuries appear minor. Medical professionals can assess and treat injuries, providing necessary care to prevent complications. Here are the critical aspects of medical attention post-crash:

- Emergency responders provide critical care at the crash scene, stabilizing injuries and transporting individuals to hospitals for further treatment.
- Depending on the severity of injuries, specialized medical care may be required. This can include consultations with specialists such as orthopedists for bone injuries, neurologists for head trauma, or chiropractors for spinal adjustments.
- Follow-up care ensures ongoing treatment and monitoring of injuries. It may involve additional medical visits, physical therapy sessions, or rehabilitation programs aimed at restoring physical function and mobility.

Timely medical attention from professionals prevents any minor health issues from worsening and ensures quick healing.

MENTAL HEALTH SUPPORT

Besides timely medical attention, you must ensure that you seek mental health support to cope with the emotional and psychological impacts of trauma. It involves seeking trauma counseling and joining support groups.

As discussed in the earlier chapters, crash-induced trauma can have various short- and long-term impacts on your mental health. Trauma counseling and therapy help cope with those issues and prevent them from turning into serious health problems and disorders.

The key aspects of trauma counseling include:

- Tailored sessions with trained counselors or psychologists focus on processing trauma, managing emotional distress, and developing coping strategies.
- Cognitive Behavioral Therapy (CBT) techniques help individuals challenge negative thought patterns and behaviors resulting from the crash, promoting emotional healing and resilience.
- Gradual exposure to traumatic memories and triggers helps desensitize individuals, reducing anxiety and fear associated with driving or accident-related memories.

In addition, joining support groups offers a valuable community-based approach to recovery, fostering empathy, understanding, and shared experiences among participants.

LEGAL ASSISTANCE

Legal assistance is crucial following a car crash to ensure you understand their rights, seek compensation for damages, and navigate complex legal processes. The important aspects of legal assistance involve consulting a lawyer and leveraging free legal consultation services.

Lawyers specializing in road crashes offer expert advice on legal options, rights, and potential claims for compensation. Initial consultations help assess the viability of a legal claim and provide clarity on the next steps.

Besides that, many law firms offer free initial consultations, making legal guidance more accessible to car crash victims. Other resources such as community support services, educational workshops, and online resources can also help you find the help and support you need to recover from the trauma.

HOW TO SUCCESSFULLY ENGAGE USEFUL RESOURCES

To leverage your support network, it is crucial to not only connect with them but also engage them in your recovery through the following steps:

IMMEDIATE ACTION

Traumatic experiences can leave you feeling vulnerable, scared, and exhausted for a long time. You must take immediate action to avoid these feelings lingering for a long time.

Here are the most important immediate action steps that help you engage with professionals and your support groups:

- Prioritize seeking medical care immediately after the crash to address any visible and internal injuries.
- Contact a lawyer for initial guidance on legal rights, potential claims, and steps to protect oneself legally.

CONTINUOUS SUPPORT

Trauma healing is an ongoing process that requires continuous professional monitoring and assistance. Ensure proper follow-up care and seek therapeutic services to accelerate your recovery. Maintain regular medical appointments for ongoing treatment and monitoring of injuries and engage in trauma counseling or support groups. These actions help you gradually manage emotional and psychological effects over time.

COMMUNITY INVOLVEMENT

Your community can be a great source of help during times following a traumatic crash. Rather than avoiding them, try to increase your engagement to seek their help. You can join local support groups or attend community workshops to connect with others who have experienced similar trauma.

Try finding non-profit organizations offering specialized trauma healing services for crash survivors, victims, and witnesses. They may also offer financial aid and advocacy, which may help you in different areas.

EDUCATIONAL PURSUITS

Besides seeking help from other resources, you must also enhance your knowledge by seeking the latest information from different educational resources. Consider attending relevant workshops and seminars to learn about new things and connect with like-minded individuals. Various community centers and legal aid clinics organize educational workshops and seminars to help survivors understand their legal rights and procedures. You can also utilize various online resources and legal websites to access informational guides, educational materials, and legal advice on crash recovery.

By taking the right immediate actions, seeking continuous support, and increasing your engagement in the community, you can effectively deal with post-trauma challenges. It not only enables you to recover quickly from your trauma but also allows you to become a helpful resource for others.

A QUICK GUIDE TO SUPPORT GROUPS

Below is a comprehensive list of resources for helping you connect with support groups tailored to your needs and establish a network of supportive individuals to help with your trauma recovery.

- Crash Support Network
- Trauma Survivors Network (TSN)
- Insurance Institute for Highway Safety (IISH)
- United Spinal Association
- Amputee Coalition
- Brain Injury Association
- Enjuris
- RoadPeace

- Motorcycle Accident Victim Support Groups
- Farah and Farah
- Car Support Network

CONCLUSION

Resorting to solitude and avoiding social interaction is a common behavior observed among trauma survivors. Although it is often considered normal, it can impact your overall life and productivity in the long term if not managed well. While the healing process begins from within, it also involves engaging with people around you and utilizing their support to facilitate your healing.

Facing people after a traumatic crash may sound challenging, but a well-planned and managed networking strategy can simplify the process and help you connect with like-minded people. Being a part of a supportive community and network provides worthwhile help and enables you to become a source of help for others around you. Adopting this approach benefits your recovery and contributes to your personal development as a responsible citizen. It also prepares you for the next steps in your recovery, which involve the implementation of advanced coping strategies for managing trauma-related stress and anxiety.

Chapter Six

ADVANCED COPING STRATEGIES

"Facing it, always facing it, that's the way to get through. Face it."

—**Conrad Joseph**

Mastering your fears requires understanding them. Regardless of how difficult it might seem to get back on the road after a crash, the only way to overcome your fears is by facing them. If you want to set yourself free from the paralyzing grip of trauma, you must identify the root causes of your fear and anxiety and address them directly. Sometimes, basic therapies and methods may work, while other times, you may need complex strategies to manage trauma-related stress and anxiety associated with driving.

Advanced coping strategies go beyond the immediate aftermath of the crash. They involve a more detailed and sustained approach to mental health and recovery. These strategies involve an in-depth understanding of the psychological and physiological mechanisms responsible for trauma-induced fear. As a result, they mitigate fear and enable you to reclaim control over your life.

COGNITIVE BEHAVIORAL THERAPY (CBT) BASICS

Cognitive behavioral therapy (CBT) is a talking therapy that can help you manage your problems by changing the way you think and behave.[16] It is a highly effective treatment method for various psychological issues, including those stemming from traumatic car crashes. This form of therapy is grounded in several core principles that aim to help individuals understand and manage their mental health challenges.

CORE PRINCIPLES OF CBT

Cognitive behavioral therapy is based on the following core principles:

Interconnectedness of Thoughts, Emotions, and Behaviors: One of the most important principles of CBT is the belief that thoughts, emotions, and behaviors are interlinked. This implies that negative thoughts can lead to distressing emotions, resulting in unhelpful behaviors. By identifying and challenging these negative thought patterns, individuals can alter their emotional responses and behaviors, breaking the cycle of distress.

Focus on the Present: Unlike some therapies that highly focus on an individual's past, CBT primarily focuses on the present, i.e.,

---

[16] Overview - Cognitive behavioural therapy (CBT) - NHS (www.nhs.uk)

current problems and situations. This forward-looking approach helps individuals deal with their immediate issues, making it particularly effective for those recovering from recent traumatic events like car crashes.

Goal-Oriented and Problem-Solving Approaches: CBT is a structured and goal-oriented approach focusing on specific problems and the possible solutions to solve them. Therapy sessions involve setting realistic and achievable goals and collaboratively working towards them. This structured approach provides a sense of direction and purpose, helping individuals measure their progress over time.

Educative Nature: CBT is also educative, equipping individuals with skills and strategies to manage their thoughts, emotions, and behaviors effectively. Clients learn to identify cognitive distortions, reframe negative thinking, and apply problem-solving techniques. This education empowers them to become their own therapists, using the tools and techniques learned in therapy to handle future challenges independently.

Time-Limited: One of the practical aspects of CBT is its time-limited nature. Unlike therapies that may continue indefinitely, CBT typically involves several sessions, often between 8 and 20, depending on the individual's needs. This makes it a cost-effective treatment option and ensures that therapy remains focused and efficient.

KEY TECHNIQUES USED IN CBT

Cognitive behavioral therapy is based on the following key techniques and strategies:

Cognitive Restructuring

This technique helps you confront the negative thoughts about the crash and its aftermath. It may involve identifying and reframing cognitive distortions into balanced and more positive thoughts. For instance, reframing "I'm never safe on the road" to "I can take precautions to be safer." It might seem like a really small thing to do, but it can help reduce PTSD symptoms.

Behavioral Activation

Behavioral activation focuses on increasing engagement in positive and meaningful activities to combat depression and improve mood. By identifying and scheduling enjoyable or important activities, individuals can break the cycle of inactivity and withdrawal that often accompanies depression. For someone recovering from a car crash, this might involve gradually reintroducing things that they once enjoyed or finding new ones that provide a sense of accomplishment and pleasure.

Exposure Therapy

Exposure therapy is a technique used to help individuals confront and reduce their fear of specific situations or stimuli. By gradually and repeatedly exposing individuals to their feared situations in a controlled and safe manner, the anxiety associated with these situations decreases over time. This technique is discussed in detail later in the chapter.

Skills Training

Skills training involves learning practical skills to manage your emotions, behaviors, and interactions effectively. This can include stress management techniques, assertiveness training, communication skills, and relaxation exercises. For instance, you may learn deep breathing exercises or mindfulness techniques to manage your anxiety, especially while driving.

Problem-Solving

Problem-solving techniques help individuals develop effective strategies to address and overcome life challenges. This involves identifying problems, generating potential solutions, evaluating the pros and cons of each solution, and implementing the chosen solution. For someone dealing with the aftermath of a car crash, this might involve figuring out how to arrange transportation, manage medical appointments, or navigate insurance claims.

Homework Assignments

Homework assignments are also an integral component of CBT, designed to reinforce and apply the skills learned during therapy sessions. These assignments allow you to practice new techniques in real-life situations, track your progress, and reflect on your experiences. Home assignments for trauma recovery may include journaling, practicing relaxation exercises, or monitoring your driving performance.

Your therapist may use a combination of these techniques to adopt a comprehensive and structured approach to healing. This approach helps you recover from the psychological impacts of traumatic car crashes while improving your overall mental health and well-being.

APPLYING CBT IN CAR CRASH TRAUMA RECOVERY

When trying to recover from a traumatic crash, Cognitive Behavioral Therapy (CBT) can be a highly effective approach for addressing the psychological repercussions of traumatic experiences. It aims to help you overcome the psychological impacts and regain your mental well-being.

Cognitive behavioral therapy facilitates trauma recovery by addressing the following conditions:

POST-TRAUMATIC STRESS DISORDER (PTSD)

Car crashes can lead to the development of post-traumatic stress disorder (PTSD), characterized by intrusive thoughts, nightmares, flashbacks, and severe anxiety. CBT can help deal with PTSD by helping you restructure your negative thoughts. It also works to reduce the emotional and physical impacts of the crash through techniques like exposure therapy and trauma-focused CBT.

ANXIETY

As discussed earlier in the book, a traumatic car crash can lead to the development of generalized anxiety symptoms and panic attacks. These symptoms can worsen when you try to drive or ride a vehicle again. Applying different cognitive behavioral techniques can help reduce your anxiety levels and help you regain your confidence.

Moreover, relaxation methods and mindfulness exercises can help manage anxiety symptoms more effectively. Once your anxiety reduces, you can leverage gradual exposure to being in a vehicle again and progressively move to challenging situations. This approach helps desensitize you to your anxiety triggers and allows you to be on the roads in full confidence like before.

DEPRESSION

Long-term anxiety can turn into depression, which results in the loss of normalcy, especially after a car crash. It may involve the accumulation of negative thoughts preventing you from easily performing your routine activities. CBT techniques help you fight the dark beliefs and thought patterns that may contribute to depression. They also motivate you to engage in activities you once enjoyed to reconnect with your former self and counteract the withdrawal and inactivity associated with depression.

Vehophobia (Fear of Driving)

Vehophobia refers to a persistent and intense fear of driving, usually developed after having or witnessing a traumatic car crash or a near-miss experience while driving. As a result, the vehophobic person may avoid riding and driving vehicles, which affects their life and daily activities. CBT focuses on starting with minimal exposure, such as sitting in a parked car, and slowly increasing to driving short distances in familiar areas. It helps reduce the fear response associated with driving and allows you to regain the confidence to get back on the road. It also involves learning defensive driving skills and strategies to feel more in control and confident while driving.

The key components of CBT used in treating car crash trauma include the following:
- Exposure Therapy
- Cognitive Restructuring
- Psychoeducation
- Stress Management Techniques
- Behavioral Activation
- Skills Training

EXPOSURE THERAPY

The American Psychological Association defines exposure therapy as *"a psychological treatment that was developed to help people confront their fears."*[17]

The therapy focuses on reducing fear and anxiety by gradually exposing an individual to the feared object, situation, or memory in a controlled and safe manner. It is based on the fundamental principle that repeated and controlled exposure can help individuals desensitize their fear response. It also helps in better anxiety management and gradually diminishing the fear.

EXPOSURE VARIATIONS

The exposure therapy may utilize the following variations of exposure depending on the specific scenario and recovery needs of an individual:

---

[17] What Is Exposure Therapy? (apa.org)

IN VIVO EXPOSURE

It involves directly facing the fear in real life, which may include a person, object, or place. For instance, someone who is afraid of driving a vehicle may be asked to drive a car on the road. If you choose to undergo in-vivo exposure, you might have to start with sitting in a parked car and eventually progressing to short drives in familiar, low-traffic areas. Direct confrontation with fear is a common therapy method for treating phobias and anxiety disorders in real life.

IMAGINAL EXPOSURE

As the name indicates, this method involves vividly imagining the feared object, person, place, or situation to reduce the feelings of fear. Instead of directly confronting your fears, it adopts a more subtle approach to acknowledge and mitigate them. It is often utilized when real-life exposure is too distressing for an individual.

For instance, a person traumatized by a crash might be asked to recall the crash scene and their emotions at that time to process and reduce its impact.

VIRTUAL REALITY EXPOSURE

Sometimes, therapists use computer-generated simulations to recreate the feared situation in a controlled virtual environment. It helps an individual to have an experience similar to real life without actually being involved in it. This method is usually utilized when in-vivo exposure is either not practical or highly distressing.

Virtual reality exposure offers a higher degree of control over the exposure and allows for a more personalized experience tailored to an individual's comfort level. For instance, a person may be exposed to driving through a realistic driving simulation involving various conditions and scenarios.

INTEROCEPTIVE EXPOSURE

Interoceptive exposure targets the physical sensations of anxiety and panic by deliberately inducing those sensations in an extremely controlled manner. This helps individuals learn that these sensations are not dangerous and can be tolerated.

For someone who experiences panic attacks related to driving, interoceptive exposure might involve exercises that mimic the physical sensations of panic, such as hyperventilation or spinning in a chair, helping them become less fearful of these sensations.

METHODS UTILIZED IN EXPOSURE THERAPY

Besides the different exposure therapy variations mentioned above, the following additional methods and strategies are used in exposure therapy.

Graded Exposure

Graded exposure involves a step-by-step approach to confronting the feared object or situation, starting with the least anxiety-provoking scenarios and gradually progressing to more challenging ones. For someone who fears driving, this might begin at a small level, like sitting in the car and adjusting in the seat while finding your comfort back to the steering wheel. From there, it can level up to driving around a quiet neighborhood and eventually driving on busier roads.

Flooding

Flooding involves immediate and intense exposure to the most feared situation without gradual build-up. This method is based on the idea that prolonged exposure will lead to a gradual decrease in anxiety over time. In the case of driving phobia, flooding might involve the individual driving on a busy highway right away, under the supervision of a therapist, until their anxiety significantly decreases.

Systematic Desensitization

Systematic desensitization combines gradual exposure with relaxation techniques. The individual learns to associate the feared situation with a relaxed state of mind instead of anxiety. A person afraid of driving might practice deep breathing or progressive muscle relaxation techniques while imagining or experiencing different driving scenarios, gradually moving from less to more anxiety-provoking situations.

HOW IT HELPS

Exposure therapy is based on the following principles and beliefs:

Habituation: When exposed to feared objects or situations for a long time, people tend to become habitual to them, and their fear completely washes off. Habituation is the process by which repeated exposure to a feared stimulus reduces the intensity of the anxiety response over time.

Extinction of Previously Learned Associations: Exposure can also help weaken previously learned associations with certain situations, objects, and activities and anxiety. For instance, a person associating driving with danger due to a past crash may develop a less fearful perception of driving after a repetitive cycle of safe driving experiences.

Self-Efficacy: Successful confrontation of fear leads to increased self-efficacy or the belief in one's ability to handle challenging situations. For instance, successfully completing a series of graded driving tasks can help you feel more confident in your ability to drive.

Emotional Processing: By repeatedly revisiting the crash scenario in a controlled manner (through direct and indirect exposure), you can process your emotions related to the event, reducing its traumatic impact and leading to emotional healing.

USING EXPOSURE THERAPY FOR TREATING CRASH-RELATED TRAUMA

Here is how you can use exposure therapy methods for treating crash-related trauma.

Real Exposure Therapy

Real-exposure therapy involves direct exposure to the feared situation or stimuli in real-life settings. For those affected by car crashes, this could mean gradually engaging in driving and then taking it further under the supervision of a therapist.

This step-by-step approach allows the person to build confidence and reduce anxiety in a controlled manner. It is important to desensitize the individual to the feared situation and help them regain confidence in their ability to drive or be in a car without overwhelming fear.

Written Exposure Therapy (WET)

Written Exposure Therapy (WET) involves writing about the traumatic event in detail, focusing on the thoughts and feelings associated with the experience. This method helps individuals process their trauma through structured writing sessions.

Participants write about their traumatic event for a set duration of time, typically guided by specific prompts or questions provided by the therapist. These writing sessions can take place in a therapeutic setting or at home, with regular follow-up sessions to discuss the written content.

To facilitate emotional processing and reduce the impact of traumatic memories by confronting and organizing them in a coherent narrative. Studies show a positive impact of written exposure therapy for dealing with crash-related PTSD.[18]

Virtual Reality Exposure Therapy (VRET)

Virtual Reality Exposure Therapy (VRET) uses virtual reality technology to simulate the feared situation in a safe and controlled atmosphere. This method is particularly effective for individuals with severe anxiety or PTSD, as it provides a highly immersive experience without real-world risks.[19]

---

[18] Written Exposure as an Intervention for PTSD: A Randomized Clinical Trial with Motor Vehicle Accident Survivors - PMC (nih.gov)

[19] Virtual Reality Exposure Therapy for PTSD symptoms after a road accident: an uncontrolled case series - PubMed (nih.gov)

Individuals are exposed to virtual scenarios that mimic the traumatic event using VR headsets and software. For car crash-related trauma, this could involve simulated driving experiences, varying from simple road conditions to more complex and anxiety-inducing situations.

To provide a realistic yet safe platform for individuals to confront their fears, practice coping strategies, and gradually desensitize them to the triggers of their trauma.

Eye Movement Desensitization and Reprocessing (EMDR)

EMDR is a therapeutic approach primarily used to treat PTSD and trauma-related disorders. The technique has shown effective results in reducing anxiety levels in PTSD patients.[20] It involves a specific eye movement while recalling and processing traumatic memories.

For instance, a therapist may ask an individual to focus on a specific object, such as a moving pendulum, while recalling their traumatic experience.

If you are wondering how it works, here are the details:

Bilateral Stimulation: EMDR involves bilateral stimulation, which can be achieved through eye movements, taps, or auditory tones. This bilateral stimulation is thought to engage both hemispheres of the brain, facilitating the processing of traumatic memories.

---

[20] Frontiers | Eye Movement Desensitization and Reprocessing and Slow Wave Sleep: A Putative Mechanism of Action (frontiersin.org)

Adaptive Information Processing (AIP) Model: According to the AIP model, EMDR helps reprocess traumatic memories by fostering adaptive information processing. This means that disturbing memories can be integrated into existing neural networks more effectively through bilateral stimulation.

Working Memory Theory: EMDR utilizes working memory theory, which suggests that engaging in bilateral stimulation while recalling distressing memories may reduce the vividness and emotional intensity of those moments. This process allows individuals to process and make sense of their traumatic experiences in a better way.

Physiological Changes: EMDR is believed to induce physiological changes that reduce emotional distress. This may include changes in heart rate variability, cortisol levels, and other stress-related physiological markers.

EMDR is believed to affect brain function by engaging bilateral stimulation, which involves eye movements, taps, or auditory cues. This stimulation is thought to facilitate communication between different parts of the brain, promoting adaptive processing of traumatic memories.

Clinical studies and observations suggest that EMDR can significantly reduce symptoms of PTSD, anxiety, and depression in individuals who have experienced traumatic events such as car crashes.[21] It is often reported to lead to symptom relief and improved emotional processing over time.

---

[21] The Use of Eye-Movement Desensitization Reprocessing (EMDR) Therapy in Treating Post-traumatic Stress Disorder—A Systematic Narrative Review - PMC (nih.gov)

EMDR for the Treatment of Traffic Crash-Related Trauma and PTSD

Since clinical studies and observations support the use of EMDR for treating trauma and PTSD, it can be used for the treatment of car crash-related trauma and PTSD. Several studies emphasize the effectiveness of EMDR in reducing crash-related trauma symptoms.[22]

Dual Attention Tasks and Bilateral Stimulation

EMDR therapy involves dual attention tasks, where you simultaneously focus on a distressing memory and bilateral stimulation (e.g., eye movements). This process can facilitate the reprocessing of traumatic memories and the integration of new, more adaptive information.

Meta-Analytic Evidence

Meta-analytic studies have supported the efficacy of EMDR in treating PTSD and trauma-related disorders across various populations. These analyses compile data from multiple studies to assess overall treatment effects and confirm the therapeutic benefits of EMDR.

EMDR 2.0 Group Protocol

EMDR 2.0 protocols often involve group settings where individuals with similar traumatic experiences participate in therapeutic sessions together. This approach aims to enhance treatment outcomes through shared experiences, peer support, and structured therapeutic interventions.

---

[22] Dnb-33_S-1_SVE.pdf (psychiatria-danubina.com)

Comprehensive Treatment Phases

EMDR typically involves a structured approach with several phases, including history-taking, preparation, assessment, desensitization, installation, body scan, closure, and reevaluation. Each phase is designed to systematically address and process traumatic memories while ensuring the client's safety and well-being.

Long-Term Coping Mechanisms

Besides dealing with the underlying symptoms of trauma and anxiety, you must develop a long-term coping mechanism to sustain the positive impacts of your recovery strategies. Right below are some effective coping mechanisms that can help enhance and maintain your recovery outcomes.

EMOTION-FOCUSED COPING MECHANISMS

Emotion-focused coping involves strategies aimed at managing the emotional distress caused by trauma, such as those resulting from car crashes.

These strategies can include:

Seeking Emotional Support: As discussed in the previous chapter, social support can significantly affect your trauma healing and recovery. Engage with family, friends, or support groups to express emotions and receive comfort and understanding. This builds on the importance highlighted in previous discussions about the role of social support in recovery.

Religion and Spiritual Practices: For many individuals, faith and spiritual practices also provide comfort, meaning-making, and resilience in the emotionally draining days of trauma. Spiritual beliefs and rituals can help individuals find solace and cope with difficult emotions.

RESILIENCE BUILDING

Resilience refers to the ability to bounce back from adversity and maintain well-being despite facing significant life challenges.[23] Building resilience after a traumatic event, especially after a car crash, involves active coping beliefs, attachment, and social connections.

Adopting positive beliefs about your ability to cope and overcome difficulties can include cultivating a sense of optimism, self-efficacy, and adaptive thinking patterns. Strengthening relationships with supportive others, such as family, friends, or community members, provides emotional stability and a sense of belonging, which are crucial for long-term resilience.

LIFESTYLE ADJUSTMENTS

This technique will be covered in-depth in the next chapter. However, here is an overview of key lifestyle changes you must make for better and long-term outcomes.

Regular Physical Activity: Regular physical activity is essential for effective trauma healing and recovery. Exercise offers various worthwhile benefits, including mood regulation, reduced anxiety and depression, improved sleep, and better overall physical health.

---

[23] Risk and resilience factors of persons exposed to accidents - PMC (nih.gov)

Healthy Diet: A balanced diet rich in nutrients supports both physical and mental health. Consuming a variety of foods, including fruits, vegetables, lean proteins, and whole grains, provides essential vitamins and minerals that aid in recovery and boost energy levels.

Adequate Sleep: Quality sleep is vital for cognitive function, emotional regulation, and physical recovery. Good sleep hygiene practices can improve sleep quality and overall well-being. They include consistent practices such as maintaining a consistent sleep schedule and creating a relaxing bedtime routine.

These lifestyle adjustments support trauma recovery and contribute to long-term resilience and well-being.

MINDFULNESS AND MEDITATION

Mindfulness involves paying attention to the present moment without judgment. It can help individuals manage stress, reduce pressure, and improve overall emotional, physical and mental health. Techniques such as mindful breathing, body scans, and mindful walking can be incorporated into daily routines to foster a sense of calm and awareness.

EXPRESSIVE TECHNIQUES

The recovery techniques allow you to express yourself through verbal and non-verbal means to relieve anxiety and internal tension associated with depression. For instance, the following expressive methods can be effective in providing you with relief from trauma-induced anxiety.

Journaling: Writing about thoughts and feelings related to the traumatic event can be a powerful way to process emotions and gain insights. Journaling provides a safe space to express and reflect on your experiences, which can help make sense of the trauma and identify patterns of thought and behavior.

Art Therapy: Engaging in creative activities such as drawing, painting, gardening, craftwork, or sculpting can be a therapeutic outlet for expressing emotions that may be difficult to articulate with words. Art therapy can facilitate emotional release, reduce stress, and promote healing by tapping into the subconscious mind.

AVOIDANCE OF NEGATIVE COPING STRATEGIES

Sometimes, the trauma can lead to such overwhelm and anxiety that you may resort to negative coping strategies as a way to numb your pain or to seek an escape from the persistent negative emotions. While these strategies may provide you with a momentary escape from your anxiety, they can have disastrous impacts on your overall health in the long term.

This approach can lead to a range of additional problems, including over-dependency, deteriorating physical health, and exacerbated mental health issues. It is crucial to avoid negative coping strategies such as smoking or substance abuse. Additionally, you must seek healthier alternatives and coping strategies.

Instead of resorting to substances, consider engaging in positive coping strategies, such as those mentioned earlier, including mindfulness practices, expressive techniques like journaling and art therapy, and seeking support from family, friends, or professional counselors. These methods can help manage and alleviate emotional distress constructively, promoting long-term recovery and well-being. You can create a more stable and supportive foundation for your recovery by consciously avoiding negative coping techniques and incorporating positive ones.

These long-term coping mechanisms and resilience-building strategies are essential for individuals recovering from trauma, including the psychological effects of car crashes. They promote emotional healing, enhance adaptive coping skills, and foster a sense of hope and empowerment in the recovery process.

CHECKLIST FOR COGNITIVE BEHAVIORAL TECHNIQUES

Below are some of the techniques that have been proven to be effective in addressing the long-term impact of traffic crash-related trauma. Use this checklist to leverage different cognitive behavioral techniques for addressing trauma-related psychological and behavioral issues:

- ☐ Cognitive Restructuring or Reframing
- ☐ Guided discovery
- ☐ Exposure therapy
- ☐ Journaling and thought records
- ☐ Behavioral experiments
- ☐ Activity scheduling and behavioral activation
- ☐ Role-playing
- ☐ Relaxation techniques and mindfulness
- ☐ Problem-solving

- ☐ Graded exposure
- ☐ Cognitive pie chart
- ☐ ABC technique

CONCLUSION

In our lives, most of the time, internal fear and anxiety do more harm to us than the apparent traumatic experience. For instance, after a car crash, you might not want to sit in the car again, let alone ride it. Why it happens? All because of the fear settled in your heart, hindering your life and daily tasks. Dealing with this fear requires understanding, processing and eliminating it. Advanced coping strategies such as cognitive behavioral therapy, exposure therapy, eye movement desensitization and reprocessing (EMDR) can play a significant role in helping you overcome your fears. These strategies involve gradual, controlled exposure to the source of your fear while addressing other fear-induced symptoms to help you overcome it.

Additionally, incorporating mindfulness and relaxation techniques can significantly aid in managing anxiety. Practices such as deep breathing, progressive muscle relaxation, and mindfulness meditation can help calm your mind and reduce the physical symptoms of stress. At the same time, it is essential to engage in regular physical exercise, maintain a healthy diet, and ensure adequate sleep, as it is crucial in bolstering your overall resilience and well-being. Adding these strategies to your trauma recovery toolkit provides you with a comprehensive and holistic approach to long-lasting recovery outcomes.

Part Four
EXPAND AND EMPOWER

Chapter Seven

LIFESTYLE ADJUSTMENTS FOR SUSTAINED RECOVERY

"The truth is, unless you let go, unless you forgive yourself, unless you realize that the situation is over, you cannot move forward."

—**Steve Maraboli**

Adjusting your lifestyle is not about limitations but about building a new foundation. If you have been through a car crash, you would know better how life feels after that incident, and you cease to feel your normal self. Even if you do not recall the event daily or try to avoid triggers, its psychological impacts hinder your routine, impacting everything you do. While you may be attending therapy sessions and practicing coping strategies, adjusting your lifestyle can significantly improve your overall healing progress.

By lifestyle adjustments, I do not refer to turning your life upside down with extensive changes. However, adjusting your lifestyle to supplement your recovery involves gradually adopting the healthy activities that are essential for your overall well-being. It is about creating a supportive environment around yourself that nurtures your physical, emotional, and mental well-being. It is about making the right daily choices to ensure that everything you do brings you back to your normal and even better self. It all starts with establishing and following a routine.

IMPORTANCE OF ROUTINE

If someone mentions trauma healing, you may think about therapy sessions, exercises, medication, and counseling. This is what a usual trauma-healing approach looks like. However, I want to disclose that the holistic trauma healing approach extends way beyond these activities. Although they are crucial to your healing, they represent only one side of the picture. On the other hand, there are vital changes to your day-to-day life that can make a tremendous difference to your life than you may think.

You may have heard about the significance of a routine for time management and other goals. However, it can also play an instrumental role in your recovery. The benefits of establishing and following a routine have far-reaching impacts on trauma healing.

PSYCHOLOGICAL STABILITY AND PREDICTABILITY

Stress is one of the most common triggers of PTSD, and exposure to stressful situations can bring back the unpleasant memories of your traumatic experience. Following a good routine can significantly reduce stress levels and provide psychological stability. The predictability of a routine allows you to accept and handle a situation better without stressing out unnecessarily.

Having psychological stability and predictability are also crucial in the aftermath of a traumatic event like a car accident. You may have heard about it that the human mind thrives on patterns and consistency. We usually tend to work well in a predictable environment. A routine offers a sense of normalcy and order amidst the chaos. Knowing what to expect each day can reduce anxiety and stress, allowing you to focus more on recovery. This stability helps anchor your thoughts and emotions and gives you an ideal state of mind for healing.

REDUCTION OF PTSD SYMPTOMS

Routine plays a significant role in mitigating PTSD symptoms. A balanced way of living usually includes a sleep schedule, meal plan, and dedicated time for exercise and other routine tasks. This time allocation provides you with a sense of consistency and certainty that, in turn, helps in reducing the common PTSD symptoms.

Structured daily activities can distract the mind from intrusive thoughts and flashbacks, reducing their frequency and intensity. By engaging in consistent, purposeful tasks, you create positive mental and physical distractions that can lessen the grip of trauma-related memories. Moreover, routines help in establishing sleep patterns and reducing insomnia, a common PTSD symptom, thereby enhancing overall mental health.

ENHANCED EMOTIONAL REGULATION

Emotional regulation is about moving on and not letting your emotions hold you back from doing important things. When you have a defined routine, you have a virtual planner in your mind, informing you of what to expect. This balanced environment enables you to manage your emotions efficiently. Regular activities such as exercise, mindfulness practices, and engaging in hobbies help stabilize mood swings and reduce irritability. Knowing what to expect in your day makes preparing yourself mentally and emotionally easier. It maintains an equilibrium and reduces emotional outbursts or feelings of helplessness.

ESTABLISHING A SENSE OF CONTROL

Trauma often leaves individuals feeling powerless and out of control. A routine can counteract these feelings by reinstating a sense of agency and autonomy over your life. Planning and adhering to a daily schedule allows you to make decisions and assert control over your environment, which is empowering and essential for psychological recovery. This regained control can significantly boost your confidence and self-worth, aiding in the healing process in the long run.

BUILDING SELF-EFFICACY

Self-efficacy is your firm belief in your ability to manage and succeed in specific situations. This belief is crucial for recovery. A routine helps build this belief by setting achievable goals and providing a sense of accomplishment. Completing daily tasks, no matter how small, reinforces your capability and resilience. This continuous reinforcement builds self-efficacy, encouraging you to take on more significant challenges and gradually rebuild your life post-trauma.

SUPPORTING PHYSICAL HEALTH

Physical health is closely linked to mental well-being, and a routine can significantly enhance your physical health. Regular exercise, balanced meals, and sufficient rest are vital components of a healthy lifestyle that can be structured into your routine. Physical activity releases endorphins, which are natural mood lifters, and then maintaining a healthy diet provides the necessary nutrients for overall health. Adequate sleep helps in body repair and mental recovery, making routine essential for holistic healing.

FACILITATING PROFESSIONAL THERAPY

A structured routine can also facilitate professional therapy by ensuring consistency and commitment to treatment plans. Regular therapy sessions, medication schedules, and follow-up appointments can seamlessly integrate into your daily life. This integration ensures that you are consistently working towards recovery with the guidance of professionals. Moreover, routines can include therapeutic activities recommended by your therapist, such as journaling, mindfulness exercises, or specific physical therapies, thereby enhancing the effectiveness of professional interventions.

PHYSICAL ACTIVITY AND TRAUMA RECOVERY

Studies show that an individual's physical and mental health is directly correlated with the level of physical activity before and after traumatic events.[24] You can use physical activity as an effective measure to improve individual mental health after traumatic events. The

---

[24] Relationship between physical activity and individual mental health after traumatic events: a systematic review - PMC (nih.gov)

physiological and psychological benefits of physical activity facilitate the trauma recovery process.

PSYCHOLOGICAL BENEFITS

The psychological benefits of physical activity include a positive impact on mood and emotional regulation. Several studies highlight the beneficial effects of physical activity on mood in both healthy and clinical populations.[25] They also suggest that physical activity may benefit psychological symptoms, such as depressive mood, in those with post-traumatic stress disorder (PTSD). Various types of exercises have been found effective as a supplementing treatment option besides trauma-focused therapy options.

While exercising offers various psychological benefits, you must understand that it does not provide a way to run away from your problems. Instead, it enables you to face and overcome them without giving in to them. Regular physical activity can release important neurotransmitters, improving your mood significantly. The major neurotransmitters released during exercise include dopamine, endorphins, and endocannabinoids. These hormones release a feeling of pleasure and relaxation and allow you to feel good. This is a natural and accessible way to manage emotional distress.

PHYSIOLOGICAL BENEFITS

Besides the psychological benefits, the physiological benefits of physical activity are also lucrative. According to the World Health Organization, physical activity contributes to the prevention and

---

[25] Frontiers | The Impact of Aerobic Exercise on Mood Symptoms in Trauma-Exposed Young Adults: A Pilot Study (frontiersin.org)

management of non-communicable diseases such as cardiovascular diseases, cancer, and diabetes, reduces symptoms of depression and anxiety, enhances brain health, and can improve overall well-being.[26] Regular exercise strengthens the heart, lungs, and muscles, enhancing the body's overall defense against stressors.

Trauma can often disrupt your body's equilibrium, so it is crucial to keep your body moving to maintain its equilibrium. Physical activity regulates the "fight and flight" response to restore the body's natural equilibrium. It, in turn, reduces the chronic stress responses that can exacerbate trauma-related symptoms. Moreover, physical fitness can improve sleep patterns, boost energy levels, and enhance overall well-being, which are very important for recovery.

When doing physical activity, ensure that you choose a tailored and supportive environment. Usually, home and non-gym environments are preferable to provide you with a relaxed and peaceful workout environment. However, you can also opt for a gym if you are comfortable working out there.

LONG-TERM AND INTEGRATED APPROACHES

Integrating physical activity with other therapeutic approaches can enhance the effectiveness of trauma recovery programs. For instance, combining physical exercise with cognitive-behavioral therapy (CBT), mindfulness practices, or other therapeutic interventions discussed in previous chapters can provide a more holistic recovery strategy.

---

[26] Physical activity (who.int)

Physical exercise is non-invasive and can be immediately implemented as part of a comprehensive recovery program. Its multifaceted benefits address both the physical and psychological aspects of recovery, making it a valuable component of a long-term healing process.

By incorporating physical activity into daily routines, you can create a balanced recovery approach that supports mental and physical health. It enables you to overcome the challenges posed by traumatic experiences effectively.

EFFECTIVE PHYSICAL ACTIVITIES FOR TRAUMA RECOVERY

While physical activities can significantly affect your overall health and wellness and trauma recovery, some exercises might be more effective than others. If you are new to incorporating physical activity for effective trauma recovery, I recommend trying the following exercises:

YOGA

Yoga is a highly effective physical activity for trauma recovery due to its emphasis on mindfulness, controlled breathing, and gentle movement. The practice of yoga helps calm the nervous system and reduce stress hormones, promoting relaxation and mental clarity. Specific forms of yoga, such as trauma-sensitive yoga, are designed to accommodate the unique needs of trauma survivors, offering a safe space to reconnect with the body. Yoga's focus on the mind-body connection makes it an excellent choice for fostering emotional and psychological healing alongside physical wellness.

AEROBIC EXERCISES

Aerobic exercises, such as running, cycling, swimming, and brisk walking, are beneficial for trauma recovery as they increase heart rate and promote cardiovascular health. These activities boost the release of endorphins, which can alleviate symptoms of depression and anxiety. Regular aerobic exercise improves overall mood and energy levels, helping individuals manage the emotional aftermath of a traumatic event. The repetitive and rhythmic nature of aerobic exercise can also provide a meditative effect, helping to calm the mind and reduce intrusive thoughts related to trauma.

STRENGTH TRAINING

Strength training, which includes weightlifting, resistance band, and bodyweight exercises, helps build muscular strength and endurance. This form of exercise can be empowering for trauma survivors, as it enhances physical strength and a sense of control over one's body. Strength training also helps regulate the body's stress response by stabilizing the production of stress hormones and improving sleep quality. Additionally, the focus and discipline required in strength training can help divert attention from distressing thoughts and foster a sense of achievement and resilience.

DANCE AND MOVEMENT THERAPY

Dance and movement therapy is a powerful tool for trauma recovery that combines physical activity with creative expression. This is a relatively easier activity to perform each day without feeling overwhelmed. This form of therapy further allows you to express emotions and experiences that might be difficult to articulate verbally.

Dance therapy's rhythmic and dynamic movements can help release tension and improve emotional regulation. Participating in dance and movement therapy in a group setting can also enhance social connectedness. You can also build a supportive community for your recovery by performing this activity in a group setting.

SPORTS

Whether team-based or individual, engaging in sports offers numerous benefits for trauma recovery. Sports promote physical fitness, coordination, and discipline while providing opportunities for social interaction and teamwork. Being part of a sports team can help you develop a sense of belonging and support, which is crucial for emotional healing. The competitive and goal-oriented nature of sports can also help individuals build resilience, focus, and determination, which are valuable traits in overcoming the challenges of trauma recovery.

Consider incorporating these fun and effective physical activities into your routine to enhance your healing outcomes. You can customize your routine according to your preferences, comfort, and healing needs. Creating a balanced routine with a combination of different activities is a better approach to keep you engaged and motivated. Regardless of your workout routine, stay consistent and keep going. You will surely see its impacts on your physical and mental well-being.

INCORPORATING MINDFULNESS INTO YOUR PHYSICAL ACTIVITY ROUTINE

While physical activity is beneficial for your physical and mental health, you can enhance its impacts further by integrating mindfulness into it. Evidence-based research highlights the positive impacts of combining physical activity with mindfulness for improved mental well-being.[27]

Consider adopting the following practices to incorporate mindfulness into your physical activity routine.

CHOOSE MINDFUL MOVEMENT PRACTICES

Select physical activities that naturally lend themselves to mindfulness, such as yoga, tai chi, or walking meditation. These practices emphasize a slow, deliberate pace and encourage a deep connection between mind and body. They provide a foundation for integrating mindfulness into your movement routine, helping you stay present and engaged.

FOCUS ON BREATHWORK

Incorporate breathwork into your physical activities by paying attention to your breathing patterns. Whether doing yoga, running, or lifting weights, synchronize your movements with your breath. Deep, rhythmic breathing can help regulate your nervous system, reduce stress, and maintain a sense of calm and control during your workouts.

SET AN INTENTION

Begin each session by setting a clear, positive intention. This could be a simple affirmation or a specific goal you wish to achieve during your activity. Setting an intention helps you stay focused and provides

---

[27] Effects of combining physical activity with mindfulness on mental health and wellbeing: Systematic review of complex interventions - ScienceDirect

a sense of purpose, making your physical activity more meaningful and aligned with your recovery journey.

PRACTICE NON-JUDGMENT

Adopt a non-judgmental attitude towards yourself and your progress. Recognize that trauma recovery is a gradual process and that each step forward is valuable, no matter how small. Avoid comparing yourself to others or setting unrealistic expectations. This can have detrimental impacts on your recovery. Be kind to yourself and embrace your journey with self-compassion. Make a habit of celebrating your efforts and achievements to keep yourself motivated. This practice is the key to achieving your long-term goals in your personal and professional life.

USE INVITATIONAL LANGUAGE

When guiding yourself through physical activities, use invitational language that encourages exploration and self-discovery. For instance, phrases like "if it feels right," "when you're ready," or "explore this movement" encourage you to listen to your body and make choices that feel safe and comfortable. This approach fosters a sense of autonomy and trust in your body's wisdom. You can say these phrases out loud or repeat them in your mind. This self-assurance will keep you engaged and prevent weariness.

INCORPORATE MINDFUL PAUSES

When it comes to a balanced physical activity routine, rest is as important as exercise. Take mindful pauses throughout your activity to check in with yourself. These pauses can be brief moments of stillness where you observe your breath, notice sensations in your body, or reflect on your emotional state. Mindful pauses help you stay grounded and present, enhancing your overall mindfulness practice and supporting your trauma recovery.

ENGAGE IN BODY SCANNING

Practice body scanning during your physical activities to cultivate greater body awareness. A body scan involves systematically focusing on different parts of your body, noticing any sensations, tension, or areas of relaxation. This technique helps you tune into your body's signals, promoting relaxation and a deeper connection with yourself.

SEEK TRAUMA-INFORMED GUIDANCE

Consider seeking guidance from professionals trained in trauma-informed care, such as therapists, yoga instructors, or fitness trainers who understand the nuances of trauma recovery. Trauma-informed professionals can provide tailored support and create a safe environment for your physical activities, ensuring that your practice aligns with your recovery goals and needs.

Incorporating these mindfulness techniques into your physical activity routine can create a holistic and supportive approach to trauma recovery. Mindful movement enhances your physical well-being and nurtures emotional and psychological healing. As a result, you can build resilience and reclaim a sense of balance and control in your life.

NUTRITION, SLEEP, AND TRAUMA RECOVERY

Your physical and mental health are significantly impacted by what you eat and how you sleep. However, our body also needs a list of different nutrients to keep us healthy and active. A slight disturbance in the required nutrient level in the body can lead to dire consequences, especially when one is on his way to trauma recovery.

NUTRITIONAL NEEDS AND PTSD

Nutrition plays a crucial role in supporting trauma recovery by addressing both physical and psychological health. Essential nutrients can influence brain function, mood regulation, and overall well-being, especially for individuals experiencing PTSD.

Proteins: Proteins are essential for repairing tissues and producing neurotransmitters. They also contribute to emotional stability and mental clarity. Foods rich in lean meats, fish, beans, and nuts provide the amino acids necessary for neurotransmitter synthesis, which is vital for managing stress and maintaining a balanced mood.

Antioxidants: These compounds help combat oxidative stress and inflammation, which are often elevated in individuals with PTSD. Foods high in antioxidants, such as berries, nuts, and green leafy vegetables, can help protect the brain and support mental health.

Vitamin C: Known for its role in immune function and antioxidant protection, Vitamin C also supports the synthesis of neurotransmitters and can help reduce symptoms of anxiety and depression. Citrus fruits, strawberries, and bell peppers are excellent sources.

Omega-3 Fatty Acids: Found in fatty fish, flaxseeds, and walnuts, omega-3s have anti-inflammatory properties and are associated with improved mood regulation and cognitive function. They can help reduce symptoms of PTSD and support overall mental health.

Zinc: This mineral is crucial for brain function and immune health. Zinc deficiencies have been linked to mood disorders and cognitive impairments. Foods such as lean meats, shellfish, and legumes can help maintain adequate zinc levels.

These essential nutrients are easily found in food items you consume every day. All you need to do is create a balanced meal plan to ensure you take adequate essential nutrients daily. You may seek professional help from an expert to plan your meals if you want. This minor change will positively impact your health and mood.

FIBER INTAKE AND PTSD

Besides other nutrients, fiber intake is believed to have a more significant impact on lowering PTSD levels. Research shows that the consumption of dietary fiber leads to lower levels of psychological distress.[28] Adequate fiber intake supports digestive health, which can indirectly affect mental well-being. A healthy gut microbiome is associated with improved mood and reduced anxiety. High-fiber foods such as whole grains, fruits, and vegetables can help regulate digestion and support overall health.

A good option to increase your dietary fiber intake is by incorporating a Mediterranean diet into your routine. The Mediterranean diet, rich in fruits, vegetables, whole grains, lean proteins, and

---

[28] Consumption of Dietary Fiber in Relation to Psychological Disorders in Adults - PMC (nih.gov)

healthy fats, is particularly beneficial for trauma recovery. This diet emphasizes nutrient-dense foods and is associated with reduced inflammation, better mood stability, and improved cognitive function. Its emphasis on healthy fats, such as olive oil, and a high intake of antioxidants supports both physical and mental health.

Foods to include in your Mediterranean diet include vegetables, fruits, legumes, whole grains, eggs, dairy, healthy fats, fish, and seafood. Moreover, foods to avoid in a Mediterranean diet include added sugar, refined grains, trans fat, and highly processed food. The ideal beverages include adequate amounts of water, fresh fruit juices, coffee or tea, and small amounts of red wine. You must avoid beer and liquor, drinks with added sugars, and sugar-sweetened beverages.

SLEEP DISTURBANCE AND PTSD

Sleep disturbances are common among individuals with PTSD and can exacerbate symptoms of anxiety, depression, and hyperarousal. Poor sleep quality affects the body's ability to recover and process trauma, leading to increased stress and emotional distress. Remember that no amount of mental health exercises or therapy sessions can make up for the damage caused by inadequate or poor-quality sleep. If you struggle to fall asleep or fail to take proper, good-quality sleep daily, you may need to implement some sleep quality improvement strategies.

Sleep Quality Improvement Strategies

The following strategies help improve your sleep quality and support your recovery:

- **Maintaining a Regular Sleep Schedule:** Consistency in your sleep routine helps regulate your internal body clock. Going to bed and waking up at the same time every day can improve the quality and duration of sleep.
- **Creating a Safe and Comfortable Sleep Environment:** A sleep-friendly environment includes a comfortable mattress and pillows, a cool and dark room, and minimal noise. Ensuring that your bedroom is a sanctuary for rest can enhance your sleep quality.
- **Engaging in Relaxing Activities Before Bed:** Activities such as reading, gentle stretching, or listening to calming music can signal your body that it's time to wind down. Avoiding stimulating activities, such as using electronic devices, can also help prepare your body for restful sleep.
- **Proper Sleep Hygiene:** Good sleep hygiene involves maintaining a consistent bedtime routine, avoiding caffeine and heavy meals before bed, and creating a relaxing pre-sleep routine. Implementing these practices can improve sleep onset and quality.

By addressing nutritional needs and implementing effective sleep strategies, individuals recovering from trauma can support their overall well-being, enhance their resilience, and improve their capacity to manage PTSD symptoms.

A CHECKLIST FOR HEALTHY LIFESTYLE ADJUSTMENTS

If you are on your way to recovery, the following checklist may help you keep track of your routine and adjust it accordingly to gain your desired outcomes.

Physical Health
- ☐ Regular exercise
- ☐ Healthy diet
- ☐ Adequate sleep
- ☐ Limit alcohol and caffeine

Mental and Emotional Well-being
- ☐ Mindfulness and relaxation practices
- ☐ Engaging in enjoyable activities
- ☐ Social Connections

Personal Development
- ☐ Self-compassion
- ☐ Stress management
- ☐ Journaling

Safety and Stability
- ☐ Creating a safe environment
- ☐ Routine

Education and Awareness
- ☐ Learn about trauma and recovery

Community Engagement
- ☐ Volunteer

Professional Guidance
- ☐ Regular check-ins with healthcare providers

This checklist is only to help you track your progress and not to stress out. Remember that you might not be able to check all the boxes every time, but it is alright. What matters is your efforts, even if they are little. The more consistent you are in your efforts, the better you will feel, and the quicker you will be able to recover from your trauma.

CONCLUSION

Remember that adopting a balanced routine and adopting a better and healthier lifestyle is not about limitations, as people often perceive. It is about making conscious decisions to spend most of your day doing things that take you a step closer to your goal of trauma-free living. It does not have to be something hectic that always keeps you on your toes or gets on your nerves every time you think about it. Instead, it is about bringing the seemingly small changes in your life that deeply impact you and your recovery.

From your eating habits to your sleep schedule and workout routine, everything must be aimed at improving your health without overwhelming you. This is only possible when you are truly committed and highly motivated to take action for yourself. There would be days when you may feel too lazy to move or too convinced to skip your schedule. Making the right choice at such moments goes a long way in your recovery.

Lastly, you must not forget that setbacks are a part of the process, and no one is immune from them. However, a setback is a sign of progress and shows that the effort is being made to build a better future. Once you cultivate this mindset, your journey will be significantly easier.

Chapter Eight
NAVIGATING SETBACKS

"Brick walls are not there to keep us out; they are there to show us how much we want something."
—**Randy Pausch**

Every setback is a setup for a comeback. In the recovery journey, hindrances are not only inevitable, but they are integral. When trying to overcome our fears and set our lives free from the bounds of the anxiety that grapples with our minds, we may face some challenges that compel us to pause for a while and rethink our life decisions. Some moments test our resolve, challenge our progress, and might make or break our resilience. Although obstacles are necessary for advancement, overcoming them is not always easy.

Imagine you are well into your trauma recovery journey. You have been making significant progress—your anxiety has lessened, your sleep quality has improved, and your social life is improving. You might have even started to ride or drive cars again. Just when everything is slowly stabilizing, life may throw some challenges again, and this time, amidst the progress, it might catch you off guard. It will shake the core of your existence, and you will be unable to comprehend how to move forward. However, how you handle a setback and continue pacing ahead in the journey makes all the difference.

For instance, imagine that after seeking therapy, leveraging your network's support, and adjusting your lifestyle, you feel confident and get back on the road. You are driving to meet a friend for lunch on a bright, sunny afternoon. To reach the restaurant, you have to take a particular route you have not taken since your crash but feel ready for it. As you approach an intersection, a loud car backfires right next to you. The sudden and overwhelming sound reminds you of the crash you experienced.

At this point, your behavior decides whether you have healed or still need some work.

UNDERSTANDING SETBACKS IN TRAUMA RECOVERY

When you begin your trauma recovery journey, you must expect that the challenges and setbacks are awaiting you along with the progress. Any journey, whether it is your healing journey or any other pursuit of life, has setbacks and challenges, and it is up to you how you navigate them. While you cannot steer yourself clear of these challenges, there is a better way to handle them and prevent them from affecting your journey. It involves understanding, identifying, accepting, and managing these setbacks.

Recognizing Setbacks

Setbacks can manifest in various forms, including physical, emotional, and behavioral symptoms. Each of these symptoms indicates that something within you is being triggered or that your progress is encountering resistance.

Physical Symptoms: One of the first signs of a setback can be physical. You might notice an increased heart rate as if your body is on high alert again (recall the physical symptoms of trauma). Sometimes, fatigue can set in, making it difficult to get through your daily routines. Other common physical manifestations of re-traumatization include disturbed sleep, nightmares, and difficulty falling asleep. These common physical manifestations signal that your mind and body struggle to process the recovery journey and need more time.

Emotional Symptoms: Emotionally, setbacks can evoke a surge of strong emotions. Sadness, anger, frustration, and fear could return unexpectedly. These feelings may be intense, like experiencing the trauma all over again in your thoughts, resulting in feelings of despair or hopelessness.

Behavioral Symptoms: In terms of behavior, setbacks can lead to alterations in your interactions with the world. You may start to retreat from social interactions or steer clear of specific individuals and locations that trigger memories of the traumatic event. You might experience a significant decrease in enthusiasm for activities you used to enjoy, indicating a lack of motivation or a wish to distance yourself from possible triggers.

Understanding these symptoms is the first step in addressing setbacks. By identifying them early, you can take proactive measures to manage them before they escalate, ensuring you remain on your recovery path.

Accepting Setbacks

Once you identify your retraumatization symptoms, you must accept them to manage them. Often, trauma numbs your brain, leading you to deny the setbacks. You may think that just when everything was going right and you were moving in the right direction, how can you fall back to the same old patterns? If this thought crosses your mind, you must remember and acknowledge that recovery is not a linear process. It is a nonlinear path with several ebbs and flows where you have to progress through moments of success and setbacks.

The important thing is realizing that these setbacks, which are an integral part of your journey, are not failures but rather a normal part of the recovery process. Acceptance can be facilitated by understanding and mastering the nature of trauma and its impact on the mind and body.

Managing Setbacks

Once you accept a setback, it becomes easier to manage it effectively. An effective framework to manage setbacks is through applying these strategies:

Acknowledge Your Feelings

The first step in managing a setback is to acknowledge and validate your emotions. It is natural to feel frustrated, disappointed, or even angry when you have worked so hard and your progress seems to regress. Instead of suppressing these feelings, allow yourself to experience them fully. Acknowledging your emotions without judgment creates space for healing and prevents them from intensifying.

Reevaluate Your Goals

Setbacks can be an opportunity to reassess your recovery goals. Are your expectations realistic, given your current circumstances? Adjusting your goals to better align with your present state may be necessary. This doesn't mean lowering your expectations but rather making them more attainable, which can boost your motivation and confidence as you continue your journey.

Revisit Your Coping Strategies

When setbacks arise, revisiting and potentially revising your coping strategies is crucial. What worked in the past may not be effective now, so adapting your approach is important. Experiment with different techniques, whether it is deep breathing exercises, mindfulness practices, or reaching out to your support network. Flexibility in your coping strategies ensures that you can respond to setbacks in ways that are most beneficial to your current needs.

Practice Patience

Recovery from trauma is a marathon, not a sprint. Practicing patience with yourself and the process is essential. Setbacks can slow down your progress, but they do not negate the advances you've made. Remind yourself that healing takes time and that every small step forward counts, even if the progress is not immediately visible.

Practice Self-Compassion

One of the most powerful tools in overcoming setbacks is self-compassion. Sometimes, you may empathize with others but be harsh with yourself. Treat yourself with the same kindness and understanding that you would offer to a close friend in a similar situation. Recognize that everyone experiences setbacks and that they do not define your worth or the potential for your recovery. Practicing self-compassion creates a supportive internal environment that fosters resilience and continued healing.

When applied consistently, these strategies can transform setbacks from obstacles into opportunities for deeper understanding and growth in your recovery journey.

THINGS TO LEARN FROM SETBACKS IN TRAUMA RECOVERY

The setbacks in your healing, whether you realize them or not, can be a source of learning and enhancing your healing journey. Some of the setbacks in trauma recovery, while extremely taxing, can be some of the most valuable experiences in your healing journey. They provide crucial insights and opportunities for growth that can strengthen your overall recovery process.

Here are some important lessons to learn from these setbacks:

Insights into Your Triggers and Vulnerabilities

Sometimes, you may be unable to identify all your triggers at once. Identifying and understanding the factors that bring up the traumatic memories takes a long journey and time investment. A setback typically happens when one of the triggers is activated. As a result, it can effectively bring attention to particular triggers and vulnerabilities you may have previously overlooked or underestimated. Holistic healing requires you to control all of your triggers effectively, and controlling them begins with comprehending these triggers.

Consider every challenge an opportunity to identify the exact reason for the reaction, whether it be a specific stressor, surroundings, or internal thought process. This knowledge helps you predict and handle similar situations more effectively. It also decreases the chance of being surprised by a similar trigger. Sometimes, you might have identified and worked on a trigger, but it is not enough to help you overpower it completely.

When you face challenges, they highlight the areas where you may still be emotionally or mentally sensitive. Identifying these weak points is an essential part of dealing with them head-on.

Mental Toughness

Facing challenges can challenge your ability to bounce back and stay strong mentally. You cultivate resilience when you encounter an obstacle and persevere in your healing process. Every time you successfully tackle a problem, your belief in your capability to manage upcoming obstacles grows.

Mental strength is not about being immune to setbacks but about how you react to them. It requires developing a mentality that views setbacks as a typical aspect of the healing journey instead of an indication of defeat. This change in outlook can be empowering, enabling you to confront every hurdle with more determination and confidence in your ability to bounce back.

Additionally, mental toughness involves staying dedicated to your recovery goals, even during slow progress or temporary setbacks.

Refining Your Coping Strategies

Another positive aspect of facing setbacks in your journey is that they help you analyze the effectiveness of your coping strategies. They allow you to assess how well your current coping strategies are working. If a plan is unsuccessful in avoiding or lessening a problem, it may indicate that it requires adjustments or a new approach. This does not suggest that the strategy was fundamentally flawed; instead, it might need tweaking to align more closely with your changing requirements. Sometimes, a technique might be effective but not suitable for your situation.

For instance, if you discover that a method for dealing with anxiety is not working as well as before, a setback may inspire you to consider different methods. This could entail experimenting with new relaxation methods, participating in varied therapy approaches, or reexamining tactics that you might have neglected earlier.

Improving your coping tactics also includes understanding what was effective and what was not in dealing with the setback. By examining these factors, you can create a stronger, more flexible set of tools for upcoming obstacles. This constant process of improvement ensures that your ways of dealing with things are as efficient as they can be, preparing you better for any future challenges.

The True Value of Having an Effective Support Network

One of the things we tend to underestimate the most in our lives is the value of the people around us. From our friends and family to other community members, we often focus on our individual lives and forget their contributions to our lives. Challenging times like setbacks frequently highlight the necessity of a reliable support network. In these tough times, having the support of friends, family, or professionals can significantly impact how you deal with the setback.

A strong support system is vital for giving emotional comfort, practical help, and a feeling of belonging when dealing with challenges. In times of hardship, you genuinely appreciate the importance of a support system. This could also be a good opportunity to evaluate the effectiveness and reliability of your support system.

> *Do you have individuals in your life who offer you the assistance you require?*
>
> *Do you have any gaps in your support network that require bridging?*

Acknowledging the significance of a strong support system can motivate you to invest further in these relationships, whether it be by finding new support groups, strengthening current connections, or reassessing relationships that are not beneficial to your recovery. Having a solid support network can act as a strong foundation during your healing process, providing motivation, direction, and reassurance that you are not alone in overcoming challenges.

When setbacks arise during trauma recovery, they can be beneficial if effectively dealt with. At times, they may provide invaluable perspectives on your trauma, triggers, and recovery. You can transform obstacles into opportunities for growth on your journey to recovery by recognizing your triggers and vulnerabilities, developing mental strength, improving your coping mechanisms, and valuing the support of others.

Practical Steps for Learning from Setbacks

The real trauma healing is about finding the inner strength to keep going, no matter how difficult the journey may seem. Over time, this resilience can become one of your greatest assets in healing from trauma.

Remember to learn from every setback by implementing the following strategies:

Reflect and Analyze

The first step in learning from a setback is to take the time to reflect on what happened. This involves analyzing the situation in detail and asking yourself questions like:

- *What triggered the setback?*
- *Were there any early warning signs that I missed?*
- *How did I respond to the situation?*
- *What could I have done differently?*

Reflect on these questions for a while, and soon, you will realize the reasons for your setbacks. This realization is a success and a step forward in your journey. This self-reflection can be done through journaling, talking with a therapist, or even discussing the situation with a trusted friend. The goal is to identify patterns or behaviors that may have led to the setback so that you can address them moving forward.

Adjust Treatment or Recovery Plans

Once you have reflected on the setback, the next step is to adjust your treatment or recovery plans accordingly. This might involve revisiting your goals, altering your coping strategies, or even seeking new forms of support. For instance, if a particular therapeutic approach is no longer effective, you might explore alternative therapies to address your current needs better.

Adjusting your recovery plan does not mean starting from scratch. Instead, it is about making targeted changes to help you get back on track. This could involve setting new, more realistic goals, trying different techniques for managing symptoms, or increasing the frequency of therapy sessions. Flexibility in your recovery plan is critical to navigating setbacks effectively.

Educate Yourself and Others

When it comes to trauma healing, self-awareness is never enough. You must share your learned knowledge with others. As discussed earlier in the chapter, setbacks can sometimes help you discover various aspects of trauma and healing that you might not have otherwise discovered. They allow you to educate yourself more deeply about your healing status. Such knowledge can not only help you, but also others facing a similar situation. Educating others strengthens your learning and enables you to apply your insights more effectively in your healing journey.

When educating others, you can include your friends, family members, fellow survivors, or community members in your learning. This shared learning leads to creating a support network based on shared understanding and mutual support from your support network.

Don't Slack Off From Your Mindfulness Practices

Lastly, no matter how good or bad a situation is, your mindfulness practices can be your biggest source of support. If a setback arises, it may feel tempting to slack off your mindfulness practices, but you must not give in. Maintaining consistent mindfulness and relaxation practices becomes even more crucial during challenging times. While a setback may trigger negative emotions and thoughts, mindfulness practices help you stay grounded in the present moment.

Relaxation techniques like deep breathing, progressive muscle relaxation, or meditation can help calm your nervous system and reduce the retraumatization symptoms. In the face of a setback, you must commit to these practices even more diligently to prevent the temporary challenges from derailing your recovery.

Taking these practical steps can turn setbacks into valuable learning experiences that strengthen your recovery journey.

KEY COMPONENTS OF A TRAUMA RECOVERY PLAN

A practical action begins with a holistic plan. In order to ensure comprehensive healing and prevent retraumatization, you must develop and follow a trauma recovery plan. An effective trauma recovery plan comprises the following elements:

Individualized and Person-Centered Approach

Trauma recovery is deeply personal, and what works for one person may not work for another. An individualized, person-centered approach tailors the recovery plan to your unique needs, experiences, and preferences. This means that every aspect of the plan, from therapeutic interventions to coping strategies, is chosen based on what resonates with you and addresses your specific challenges. Your trauma recovery plan must focus on empowering you to take an active role in your recovery and making decisions that align with your values and goals.

Professional Support

Professional support is a cornerstone of any trauma recovery plan. This can include therapists, counselors, psychologists, and medical professionals who specialize in trauma and its effects. Professional support provides you with expert guidance, evidence-based treatments, and a safe space to explore and process your trauma. Regular sessions with a trauma-informed professional can help you develop coping strategies, work through difficult emotions, and monitor your progress over time.

Coping Strategies

Coping strategies are essential tools that help you manage the emotional, mental, and physical challenges associated with trauma. These strategies can include mindfulness practices, grounding techniques, journaling, exercise, and other methods that help you regain control and reduce stress. A trauma recovery plan should incorporate a range of coping strategies that you can draw upon in different situations, ensuring that you have the resources to handle both everyday stressors and more intense emotional responses.

Support System

A strong support system is crucial for recovery. This includes family, friends, support groups, and community resources that provide emotional support, encouragement, and practical help. Your support system plays a crucial role in helping you feel connected, understood, and less isolated during your recovery. It's important to cultivate relationships with empathetic, patient, and willing people to support you in your healing journey.

Safety and Trust

Establishing a sense of safety and trust is fundamental in trauma recovery. This involves creating a physical and emotional environment where you feel secure and protected. Safety and trust are also built through consistent, respectful, and transparent interactions with professionals and loved ones. When you feel safe and trust those around you, you're more likely to engage fully in your recovery process and explore difficult emotions and experiences.

Empowerment and Choice

Empowerment and choice are vital in trauma recovery, as they help you regain a sense of control over your life. This means being actively involved in decisions about your treatment, setting your own goals, and choosing the coping strategies that work best for you. Empowerment also involves recognizing and building on your strengths, which can boost your confidence and resilience. By focusing on empowerment and choice, the recovery plan helps you move from a place of feeling powerless to one of self-efficacy.

Holistic, Non-Linear Approach

Recovery from trauma is not a straightforward process, and a holistic, non-linear approach acknowledges this reality. This approach integrates various aspects of well-being, including physical, emotional, mental, and spiritual health. It recognizes that progress may come in fits and starts, with setbacks being a natural part of the journey. A holistic approach also means incorporating complementary therapies alongside traditional treatments, such as yoga, meditation, and art therapy.

Education and Awareness

Education and awareness are critical components of a trauma recovery plan. Understanding the effects of trauma on your mind and body can help demystify your experiences and reduce feelings of shame or confusion. Education also empowers you to make informed decisions about your treatment and recovery process. This can include learning about trauma, its symptoms, the different treatment options available, and the importance of self-care.

Continuous Assessment

Continuous assessment is necessary to ensure your recovery plan remains adequate and relevant to your changing needs. This involves regularly reviewing your progress, adjusting goals, and modifying strategies. Continuous assessment allows for flexibility in your recovery process, ensuring that the plan evolves as you do. It also helps identify any new challenges or issues that may arise, allowing you to address them promptly and prevent setbacks.

A trauma recovery plan incorporating these key components provides a comprehensive and adaptable framework that supports long-term healing and growth.

A CHECKLIST FOR IDENTIFYING AND MANAGING COMMON TRIGGERS FOR RETRAUMATIZATION IN RECOVERY

While every person's healing journey is unique, and the setbacks they may experience may vary greatly from others, some triggers are common among car crash survivors. It can include sensory triggers as well as events such as anniversaries or hearing about similar traumatic incidents experienced by others. Below is a checklist to help you identify and manage these triggers to avoid retraumatization in recovery.

Loud Noises: Sounds like fireworks, car backfires, loud bangs, and sirens may bring back the memories of the crash.

How to Handle
- ☐ Avoid loud noises by using earplugs, noise-canceling headphones, or staying in a quieter environment.
- ☐ Practice deep breathing or grounding exercises to calm yourself during unexpected loud noises.
- ☐ Have or find a designated safe, quiet space where you can retreat if needed.

Certain Smells: The smell of burning rubber, gasoline, specific colognes or perfumes, and hospital scents.

How to Handle
- ☐ Carry a small bottle of a calming scent, like lavender or eucalyptus, that you can sniff when encountering a triggering smell.
- ☐ When possible, avoid places or situations where you might encounter these smells.
- ☐ Focus on controlled, slow breathing to reduce the intensity of your emotional response.

Specific Locations: The crash site, hospitals, or any place that reminds you of the trauma.

How to Handle
- ☐ Work with a therapist to gradually reintroduce yourself to these locations through controlled exposure.

- ☐ Visit these locations with a trusted person who can provide emotional support.
- ☐ Practice visualizing the location as a safe place or imagine a protective barrier around yourself.

Visual Stimuli: Seeing car crashes in movies or on the road and certain visual cues like flashing lights.

How to Handle
- ☐ Use content warnings or skip scenes in movies if necessary.
- ☐ Gradually expose yourself to less intense visual stimuli with professional guidance to build tolerance.
- ☐ Shift your focus to neutral or positive environmental stimuli, using mindfulness techniques to stay present.

Anniversaries: The date of the traumatic event and significant dates related to your trauma.

How to Handle
- ☐ Be proactive about planning activities or support on these days. Consider spending time with supportive people or engaging in positive distractions.
- ☐ Create a positive ritual for these dates, such as lighting a candle, journaling, or doing something meaningful that helps you reclaim the day.
- ☐ Schedule a therapy session around the anniversary to help process any resurfacing emotions.

Traumatic Stories: The unsupervised retelling of the traumatic stories or hearing others talk about their traumatic stories can exacerbate PTSD symptoms.

How to Handle

- ☐ Use breathing or mindfulness exercises to calm symptoms of trauma when they arise.
- ☐ Listen to empathize and understand that this might be the first time the other person is sharing their story.
- ☐ Politely inform the speaker about your trauma triggers and distance yourself from such conversation if it seems unmanageable.

CONCLUSION

I have reiterated this notion several times throughout this book that trauma recovery is a complex process with its ups and downs. It is not a linear journey but a path characterized by several challenges, successes, and wins. As we welcome and acknowledge the wins in our journey, we should also be prepared for the potential setbacks. A journey without challenges indicates that there might be some problems either in your understanding or your approach. You may face some challenges when you experiment with different techniques and adjust your coping strategies according to circumstances.

These challenges or setbacks are indeed a set-up for a stronger and better comeback. These learning opportunities allow you to identify and fix the potholes in your strategy to enable a smooth sail in your journey. Every setback can become a step towards improvement if you acknowledge and manage it well. When you learn to accept setbacks as a natural part of the healing process and learn from them, your approach toward life and healing transforms.

You might not always be able to maintain a positive outlook toward every challenge and may sometimes feel overwhelmed. It is normal. Whenever this happens, take a step back, relax your mind, and analyze the whole scenario from a new lens. It will allow you to reinforce your progress and deal with the situation better.

When you learn to manage setbacks well, you can move toward the next step in your journey, which involves turning pain into purpose by using your strength and insights to uplift and empower others. Remember, real progress involves a collective perspective toward well-being and betterment. The more you help others, the better your life and recovery becomes.

Chapter Nine

EMPOWERING OTHERS: TURNING PAIN INTO PURPOSE

"There are two ways of spreading light: to be the candle or the mirror that reflects it."

—Edith Wharton

Your worst moments can fuel your greatest missions and have the ability to empower you in ways you might not have imagined. The trials you have faced, the pain you have endured, and the setbacks that once seemed impossible all hold the potential to transform your life and the lives of others.

The best way to recover from a trauma or pain is to turn adversity into your biggest source of power. Overcoming your challenges fills you with such a strength that can turn your pain into a powerful tool for change. I know it sounds lucrative and challenging at the same time, and I also know that it might leave you wondering if you are even capable of all this. But if you have been following the SAFE Road Recovery framework as defined in this book, you are in the right position to transform your pain into power.

Understanding your trauma, acknowledging it, building a support network, taking proactive recovery steps, and dealing with setbacks are all signs of your healing. These signs indicate that you have developed the mental strength to overcome your fears and are ready to leverage this strength to help others around you.

Empowering others is a step forward in your self-empowerment journey, which helps you progress in your healing and growth. One of the best ways to empower yourself and others is by sharing your story and healing journey.

SHARING YOUR STORY SAFELY AND RESPECTFULLY

While it might be difficult to revisit your traumatic memories, one way to help other trauma survivors is by sharing your story safely and respectfully. Sharing your story safely and respectfully involves using such a narrative and platform that neither offends others nor impacts your mental health.

CONSIDER YOUR MOTIVATION AND GOALS

Before sharing your story, you must reflect on your reasons or source of motivation and determine your goals. You need to clearly understand why and for whom you are sharing your story. The following questions can help you determine your goals and motivation:

- What is the message you want to convey?
- Who are you trying to reach out to?
- Which people do you want to convey your story with?
- What are the pain points of your target audience?

- How does your story relate to their pain points?
- Are you seeking catharsis for your recovery or want to provide support and inspiration to others?

Some of the common reasons trauma survivors choose to voice their stories include the following:

- **Catharsis for Your Own Recovery:** Sharing your story can be a powerful tool for processing your emotions and experiences. When you articulate your journey, you give meaning to your pain, which can facilitate deeper healing. However, it only happens when sharing your story is part of your healing process, not an impulsive reaction to unprocessed emotions.

- **Providing Support to Others:** During your healing, you might have sought strength from the stories of other trauma survivors. Now, you can use yours to support others. Your story has the potential to offer motivation and guidance to those who may be struggling with similar challenges. When you share your life experience with others, you let them know they are not alone in their journey. This can be highly empowering and encouraging for others.

- **Advocating for Road Safety:** If your trauma stems from a traffic crash, you can turn your story into a powerful advocacy tool. You may share the crash's impact on your life to raise awareness about the importance of road safety measures, encourage others to drive responsibly, and support initiatives that prevent such incidents. (This topic will be explored further in the next section.)

- -Understanding your purpose, objectives, and goals will help you craft your story according to your audience's preferences. As a car crash survivor, your target audience would probably be other people who have been through a similar experience. Understanding them and setting the right goals will help you ensure that you share your story safely and respectfully.

Choose the Right Platform

Firstly, you must choose the right platform to share your story safely and respectfully. In our digitally connected world, you may have multiple platforms available, but choosing the one that fits you best is crucial. The right platform depends on your purpose and audience. For instance, if you aim to reach a larger audience, you may opt for digital platforms such as a website, podcast, blog post, or social media. On the other hand, if you are sharing your story with a niche audience, you may prefer a comparatively small platform, such as guest posts or webinars. You can also create a website or blog dedicated to your story. Each platform has its own content format that you must follow. For instance, a blog may be more detailed, informative, and educational. Contrarily, a video may be more concise, engaging, and emotional. It also depends on your comfort level and preference. You must consider all these factors when choosing a platform and format.

Maintain Privacy

While sharing can be therapeutic, protecting your privacy and the privacy of others involved is equally important. Your story should primarily convey the impact of the trauma on your life and your healing journey rather than the details of the crash. You must avoid sharing sensitive details that could identify you or others in ways that might lead to unwanted attention or stress. While you may share these details with the concerned authorities, sharing them on a public platform can be inappropriate. You can anonymize names, locations, or specific information to maintain confidentiality while maintaining your story's details and flow.

Be Mindful of your Emotional State

Before sharing your story, you must check in with yourself to assess your emotional readiness. Are you emotionally stable and ready to voice your story? Or do you need some more time? It is important to consider and prioritize your comfort and readiness rather than doing it because others are doing the same. Sharing your story can be emotionally taxing, and it is important to ensure that you are mentally in a stable place to do so. If you find yourself overwhelmed with emotions before, during, or after sharing, it may be a sign that more personal healing work is needed before you continue. If this happens, there is nothing wrong with stepping back and taking some time for yourself before continuing.

Prepare for Reactions

When you share your story with others, they respond to it differently. You must know that people will react to your story in various ways, some supportive while others potentially triggering. They will respond to your story, and most of them will potentially not even know you as a person. Instead of taking anything personal, you must treat their responses as feedback to your story. Be prepared for various reactions, including questions, emotional reactions, or even criticism. Mentally prepare yourself for this and have a plan in place for how to handle these reactions constructively.

Use Supportive Language

When sharing your story, strive to use supportive and non-judgmental language. While prioritizing your mental wellness, you must also respect others' peace of mind. Frame your experiences in a way that acknowledges the difficulties while also highlighting the strength you have developed. Try to avoid language that may unintentionally trigger others or reinforce negative self-perceptions.

Highlight Resources

Your story must not only be a mere narrative but a source of help and support for others. Include information about resources that have helped you or might be helpful to others. This could be anything from therapy options, support groups, online forums, coping strategies, or literature that you found valuable. When you share these resources, your story transforms from a personal narrative into a helpful guide for others.

Respect the Recovery Process

Remember that the recovery process for everyone, including you, is different. What worked for you may not work for someone else, and that is okay. Respect the diversity of healing journeys and avoid presenting your experience as a one-size-fits-all solution. While you may share your resources, do it in a respectful way without being overly assertive or forceful.

Continual Learning and Adaptation

Your perspective and understanding of your experiences may change as you continue to heal and grow. Be open to revisiting and adapting your story as you gain new insights. As you continue to learn about trauma and recovery, you must also continue to improve and enhance your story to make it a valuable resource for others. This ongoing process will enrich your narrative and make it more beneficial for your audience.

Legal and Ethical Considerations

If your story involves others or touches on sensitive topics, it is integral to consider the legal and ethical implications. Ensure that you have the right to share certain details, especially if it involves legal cases or other individuals who may not want their experiences publicized. Sometimes, you may not be allowed to share specific information regarding the crash. It is better to consult with your legal professional or therapist before sharing. They will help you understand your limitations and boundaries to avoid any legal complications.

HANDLING NEGATIVE REACTIONS WHEN SHARING YOUR STORY

As mentioned earlier, when you share your story on a public platform, you can get both positive and negative responses from the audience. Whatever platform and format you may choose, people can react to it in various ways. While positive responses can be a source of motivation and encouragement for you, negative responses can be demotivating and discouraging. However, you must learn to handle negative reactions that do not deter or disappoint you.

The following strategies can help you handle negative reactions when sharing your story:

Prepare Mentally and Emotionally

Besides preparing the contents of your story and choosing the right platform, you must prepare yourself mentally and emotionally to deal with potential criticism or negative responses to your story. While your intention may be to inspire or help others, not everyone will respond positively. Anticipating this possibility allows you to brace yourself emotionally. It also reduces the impact of any criticism or unfavorable responses. Remember that people's reactions often say more about their own experiences and perspectives than about you or your story. When you are prepared in advance, you can prevent negative responses from destroying your mental peace or stressing you out unnecessarily.

Set Clear Expectations

Like your goals, your expectations must be clear, including why you share your story and what you want to achieve from it. This mental clarity can prevent you from a lot of mental hassle. For instance, when you know that your aim is to educate and inform others, you do not care about a few negative responses you may get. Moreover, it also shifts others' focus from your story toward your purpose for sharing it. Let people know the purpose of your sharing—whether it is to offer support, raise awareness, or advocate for change. This can help guide the type of feedback you receive. Clarifying your boundaries and the kind of interaction you are open to can also prevent misunderstandings and create a safer space for dialogue.

Respond with Gratitude and Openness

Sometimes, the best response to criticism can be gratitude. If you encounter criticism or negative feedback, try to respond with gratitude and openness. It can be difficult, but it saves your mental health on different levels. Thank the person for their input, even if it is difficult to hear. Acknowledging their perspective does not mean you agree with it, but it shows you are open to dialogue. This approach can diffuse tension and create an opportunity for constructive conversation with your audience.

Seek to Understand

Instead of reacting defensively, take a moment to understand where the negative reaction is coming from. Ask clarifying questions, and listen to their concerns or criticisms without judgment. Understanding their point of view may provide insights into different perspectives, which can be valuable for refining how you share your story in the future.

Filter and Focus

While it is integral to incorporate your audience's feedback to improve your narrative, you must know which feedback is worth noticing. Not all feedback will be constructive or relevant. You must filter out the noise and focus on the feedback that is helpful or insightful.

Recognize that some adverse reactions may stem from misunderstanding, personal bias, or unresolved trauma in the other person. The more you focus on the constructive elements of feedback, the more you can refine your message and delivery. Filtering and focus prevent you from getting derailed by unproductive criticism.

Maintain Your Boundaries

While it is essential to be open to feedback, maintaining your boundaries is equally crucial. If someone's reaction becomes harmful or overly intrusive, it is okay to assert your boundaries firmly and kindly. You have the right to disengage from conversations that do not serve your well-being or compromise your emotional safety. Remember, sharing your story is your choice, and you are in control of how much and to whom you share.

Reflect and Adapt

After encountering negative reactions, take time to reflect on the experience. Consider what you have learned and how you might adapt your approach. This does not mean changing your story or silencing your voice, but rather fine-tuning how you present your experiences to better reach your intended audience. Reflection allows you to grow from the experience and strengthen your resolve.

Continue Sharing

The feedback on your story must not affect your motivation and determination to share your story. Even if you get some negative reviews, you must continue sharing your narrative. The only difference the audience's feedback should make in your story must be to improve it rather than demotivating you. Adverse reactions can be discouraging, but they do not have to stop you from sharing your story. Use these experiences as opportunities to refine your narrative and build your strength.

Remember, your story has the power to help others, and the positive impact it can have far outweighs the occasional negative feedback. Continue confidently sharing, knowing your voice matters and can make a difference.

ADVOCACY IN TRAFFIC SAFETY

According to the World Health Organization, around 1.3 million people die each year in traffic crashes. Road traffic injuries are one of the leading causes of death of people aged between 5-29 years.[29] Advocacy plays a vital role in shaping societal attitudes toward driving and promoting responsible driving behavior among drivers. Advocacy in road traffic safety refers to the efforts to promote and improve practices, policies, and legislation to prevent road traffic accidents and ensure safer roads. It involves raising awareness about the importance of traffic safety, influencing policy and regulatory changes, and encouraging the adoption of best practices among drivers, policymakers, and communities.

Purpose of Traffic Safety Advocacy

Traffic safety aims to narrow the gap between knowledge and practice, influence policy and legislation, and raise awareness to change driving behaviors.

---

[29] "Activities." World Health Organization (WHO), https://www.who.int/activities. Accessed 29 Aug. 2024.

Narrowing the Gap Between Knowledge and Practice

Traffic safety advocacy can bridge the gap between what we know about safe driving practices and how you implement these practices in everyday life. Despite widespread knowledge about the dangers of distracted driving, speeding, and impaired driving, dangerous driving behaviors remain prevalent. Advocacy efforts aim to translate this knowledge into actionable change. This can be done by educating the public, pushing for stricter enforcement of traffic laws, and promoting a road safety culture.

Influencing Policy and Legislation

Effective advocacy often leads to meaningful changes in traffic laws and policies. As a traffic safety advocate, you can work to influence legislation through the following:

- Highlighting the need for updated traffic laws.
- Promoting the implementation of new safety technologies.
- Ensuring that penalties for unsafe driving behaviors are appropriately enforced.

You can also be a part of awareness campaigns for seatbelt laws, helmet requirements, or introducing lower blood alcohol concentration limits for drivers.

Raising Awareness and Changing Behaviors

Advocacy efforts are also focused on raising public awareness about the importance of road safety and encouraging behavior change.

You can strive to shift attitudes and behaviors toward safer driving practices through public service campaigns, educational programs, and community initiatives. By keeping traffic safety at the forefront of public consciousness, advocates help reduce risky behaviors on the road.

Importance of Traffic Safety Advocacy

Traffic safety advocacy is vital for the following reasons:

- It can save lives and prevent potential injuries. Road crashes are a leading cause of death and injury worldwide, and many of these incidents are preventable. Advocacy efforts help reduce the number of traffic-related fatalities and serious injuries.
- Crashes not only cause the loss of life and physical harm but also have significant economic consequences. The costs associated with traffic crashes—including medical expenses, lost productivity, and property damage—place a heavy burden on individuals, families, and society. Traffic safety advocacy helps reduce these economic costs.
- Effective advocacy in traffic safety can also support vulnerable road users by creating awareness about road safety rules and practices. Road users such as pedestrians, cyclists, and motorcyclists are at a higher risk of injury and death through traffic crashes. Safe driving practices lead to enhanced road safety and decreased loss of life and money loss due to road traffic crashes.

Your Trauma and Recovery Experience and Traffic Safety Advocacy

Your experience of trauma and recovery makes you an excellent advocate for traffic safety for several reasons. You can understand and empathize with others well since you have personally experienced the crash, the trauma, and their after-effects. Your firsthand experience of a traffic crash and its aftermath gives you a deep, personal understanding of the devastating consequences of road crashes. This lived reality allows you to speak with authenticity and empathy, making your advocacy efforts resonate more with those who may not fully grasp the impact of traffic crashes. People are more likely to engage with and listen to someone like you, who has genuinely "been there."

The emotional journey you have undertaken—dealing with fear, loss, and the challenges of recovery—allows you to connect with others who may be at risk or who have also experienced trauma. When you speak about the importance of traffic safety, it is not abstract but personal; this authenticity can inspire others to act.

The experience of trauma often ignites a strong desire to prevent others from suffering similar fates. Your recovery journey has likely deepened your understanding of the importance of road safety and motivated you to advocate for change passionately. This personal mission gives you the determination and persistence necessary to be an effective advocate, as your efforts are driven by a genuine desire to make roads safer for everyone.

By sharing your story, you can help others understand the risks they might not otherwise consider and encourage safer driving behaviors. This educational aspect of your advocacy can be instrumental in fostering a culture of road safety awareness.

HOW TO ADVOCATE FOR TRAFFIC SAFETY AS A RECOVERING/RECOVERED SURVIVOR OR WITNESS TO A TRAUMATIC TRAFFIC CRASH

Advocating for traffic safety as a recovering/recovered survivor or witness takes a lot of strength. While you may appear healed, the scars left by the trauma and the learnings, as a result, can play a significant role in helping you become an excellent advocate of traffic safety.

You can use your experience as a crash survivor or witness to a traumatic crash through the following:

Share Your Story

One of the best ways to advocate for traffic safety is by sharing your experience. You can share your story through different platforms, such as public speaking, social media, and blogs. Public speaking allows you to convey your personal experiences and the lessons you have learned from them. By speaking directly to an audience, you create a personal connection that can be more impactful than written communication. Similarly, you can engage with local communities through public speaking events to share your personal story directly with people who may have experienced similar traumas or who can influence change in their circles. Speaking at schools, local clubs, or community centers can help raise awareness and encourage others to become advocates for traffic safety. You can also use digital platforms to share your story.

Participate in Awareness Campaigns

You can join various existing campaigns to play an active role there or create your own campaign to promote awareness among the public. By joining existing traffic safety campaigns, you can tap into established organizations' resources, networks, and influence. These campaigns often have the infrastructure, funding, and expertise needed to make a significant impact, and your personal story can add a powerful human element to their efforts. However, if you have a unique perspective or specific issues you are passionate about, consider creating your own campaign. This allows you to tailor your message and approach to address the exact problems you want to solve.

Advocate for Policy Change

You can also play a crucial role in advocating for policy change to ensure traffic safety. It usually involves contacting legislators through letters, calls, or direct meetings with your local representatives. You can also share your personal story with lawmakers to make your advocacy efforts more compelling and help drive legislative change. Besides advocating for policy change, you must also actively support relevant legislation, such as bills that promote road safety or provide resources for trauma survivors. These steps can help turn your advocacy into concrete action.

Educate Others

Creating awareness and educating others is an essential element of traffic safety advocacy. You can do so by developing educational materials and hosting workshops and seminars. Developing brochures, flyers, or online content that explains the importance of traffic safety and trauma recovery can help educate others. You can distribute these materials at community events, schools, or through social media to spread awareness and provide valuable information. Visual aids and clear messaging can make complex issues more accessible, helping people understand the significance of safe driving and the impact of trauma.

Organizing workshops or seminars allows you to provide in-depth education on traffic safety and trauma recovery. Ensure these are relayed to different audiences, such as students, drivers, and healthcare professionals.

Support Victims and Families

Supporting the victims and their families is integral to traffic safety advocacy. You can volunteer with support groups and create your own support network to help others. You do not have to build an extensive network with lots of resources. Instead, your support network could be a local meet-up, an online forum, or a social media group where people can connect, share their experiences, and offer support to one another. You would know better how a supportive community offers a safe space to find comfort and strength in shared experiences.

Collaborate with Law Enforcement and Schools

As a traffic safety advocate, you can partner with law enforcement and schools to develop educational programs and safety campaigns. These initiatives can help prevent future accidents and support trauma recovery. You can also assist in creating programs that teach students and community members about the importance of safe driving practices and the long-term effects of traffic accidents. Collaborative efforts can have a broader reach and more significant impact than individual efforts.

Leverage Media and Publicity

You can leverage traditional media outlets like newspapers, radio, or television to reach a broader audience. Sharing your story through interviews, op-eds, or press releases can raise awareness about traffic safety and the importance of trauma recovery, inspiring others to join the cause. Media exposure can amplify your message and reach people who may not be accessible through other channels. It also drives public support for your advocacy efforts.

A CHECKLIST: BECOMING A TRAUMA-INFORMED ADVOCATE

Becoming a trauma-informed advocate involves educating yourself about the impacts of trauma and the strategies to cope with it in a way that helps trauma survivors recover from the impacts of trauma. Below is a checklist to provide an overview of the crucial steps you must take to become a trauma-informed advocate.

- ☐ Educate yourself on trauma and its impact
- ☐ Gain knowledge in traffic safety
- ☐ Engage with trauma-informed transportation programs
- ☐ Advocate for trauma-informed policies in traffic safety
- ☐ Develop and implement community outreach programs
- ☐ Continuous learning and collaboration
- ☐ Utilize media and technology

You can also seek help from governmental and non-profit organizations that advocate for traffic safety.

A list of organizations that advocate for traffic safety:

- National Road Safety Foundation (NRSF)
- AAA Foundation for Traffic Safety
- The American Association of Motor Vehicle Administrators (AAMVA)
- Foundation for Advancing Alcohol Responsibility (Responsibility.org)
- Governors Highway Safety Association (GHSA)
- Insurance Institute for Highway Safety (IIHS)
- International Association of Chiefs of Police
- National Association of Drug Court Professionals (NADCP)
- Global Road Safety Partnership (GRSP)
- World Health Organization (WHO)

CONCLUSION

The most significant sign of healing is when a trauma survivor begins helping others who have been through similar circumstances and traumas and shares their learnings with them. This knowledge-sharing is a sign of their healing, which improves their lives and those of others around them. When you learn to overcome the impacts of your hardships, you can become a source of inspiration and empowerment for others. Sharing your story, offering support, and becoming an advocate for those still struggling are all ways to turn your pain into a force for good. It creates a ripple effect that extends far beyond your own experience.

By sharing your journey with the world and offering a listening ear to others in need, you can uplift others in the best possible way.

This uplifting of others unconsciously lifts you higher in your healing and solidifies the impacts of your growth. Reaching this level of healing leaves you with only one last step in your SAFE Road Recovery framework—maintaining your progress.

Chapter Ten

LOOKING AHEAD- MAINTAINING MOMENTUM AND BUILDING RESILIENCE

"Momentum builds success."

—**Suzy Kassem**

Resilience is not just about avoiding the storm, but it is more about learning to dance in the heavy rain without worrying about anything and letting it affect your well-being. Life is synonymous with challenges and setbacks, and resilience is all about mastering the art of responding to these challenges without letting them reduce you in any way.

As you near the end of your recovery journey, integrating the SAFE road recovery framework into your healing, you must reflect on your progress. This understanding helps you realize that recovery is not a destination but an ongoing process.

REVISITED: LESSONS LEARNED

Throughout the book, you learned various lessons regarding the understanding and handling of trauma after a crash. To look forward to your journey to recovery as a survivor or witness to a traumatic car crash, you must revisit those lessons frequently and make them an integral part of your life.

Recognition and Acceptance

One of the foundational steps in healing is recognizing and accepting the trauma you have experienced. It involves acknowledging the event's impact on your life, both emotionally and physically. This acceptance is not about condoning what happened but rather about validating your experience and embracing the feelings that come with it. This acceptance opens the door to healing and helps you confront and process the trauma instead of suppressing or denying it.

Reaching Out for Professional Help

While self-healing might seem tempting, sometimes, you need professional assistance. Trauma can leave you feeling isolated, overwhelmed, and unsure of how to move forward. Professional help, such as therapy or counseling, provides a structured environment where you can safely explore your feelings and experiences. Moreover, it offers evidence-based techniques, such as CBT or EMDR, to help you process the trauma, reduce symptoms like anxiety or PTSD, and develop coping strategies for effective emotional management.

Building a Strong Support System

To counter the isolating impact of trauma, you need people around you. A solid support system, including friends, family, support groups, or online communities, prevents you from having to deal with the trauma alone. These connections can offer different perspectives, share coping strategies, and help you stay motivated. Additionally, being part of a supportive community can reduce feelings of isolation and help you build resilience by providing a safe space to share your thoughts and feelings without judgment.

Incorporating Helpful Routine and Physical Activity

Establishing and following a daily routine can provide structure, predictability, and the sense of control that you feel you have lost in the aftermath of trauma. Your routine must include physical activity, as exercise can reduce stress, anxiety, and depression. Furthermore, activities like walking, yoga, or swimming offer dual benefits, facilitating emotional release while improving sleep quality. A balanced routine leads to a balanced lifestyle, supporting physical and mental well-being.

Leveraging The Power of Mindfulness

Mindfulness and meditation are powerful tools in trauma recovery because they help you stay present and connected to the here and now. Mindfulness practices such as deep breathing, body scanning, and guided visualization can calm your nervous system, reduce the intensity of negative emotions, and prevent you from being overwhelmed by traumatic memories.

Patience — The Key to the Recovery Process

While you may utilize the best recovery strategy and approach, healing takes time. Trauma recovery is a journey marked by ups and downs, progress, and setbacks. To deal with these transitions, you must develop patience. It allows you to accept that healing takes time and that moving at your own pace is okay. Being patient with yourself and your journey helps you manage expectations and prevents frustration or self-criticism when things do not go as planned.

BUILDING AND MAINTAINING RESILIENCE

Resilience is the ability to bounce back from adversity, adapt to challenges, and progress despite difficulties. For trauma survivors, building and maintaining resilience is an ongoing process that requires nurturing both emotional and physical well-being.

When it comes to resilience, you must focus on emotional, physical, mental, and social aspects.

Emotional Resilience

Emotional resilience begins with accepting your emotions and knowing how they manifest in your daily life. Emotional awareness means recognizing these emotions as they arise and understanding their triggers. You can manage your reactions and challenges by becoming more attuned to your emotional state.

Quite similarly, mindfulness is crucial to building emotional resilience. Mindfulness practices provide immediate relief from stress and build long-term emotional strength by teaching you how to stay calm and centered, even in difficult situations. Keeping up with therapy also allows you to address any new challenges or emotions that may arise as you navigate your recovery journey.

Physical Resilience

Physical resilience is built on proper medical care and rehabilitation. You must receive appropriate medical attention, including physical therapy and specialized care for your injuries. Moreover, you must also adopt a healthy lifestyle and not let your trauma get in the way of a healthy and fit life.

Trauma can often lead to neglecting self-care, but it is important not to let go of regular exercise, balanced nutrition, adequate sleep, and hydration. A healthy lifestyle empowers you to recover more effectively from trauma and maintain the physical strength needed to face future challenges.

Mental Resilience

In addition to physical and emotional resilience, you must also develop mental strength to deal with the aftereffects of trauma. It involves developing cognitive flexibility through education and preparedness. Understanding what to expect can alleviate fears and uncertainties, helping you to manage your mental health proactively.

Cognitive flexibility allows you to adjust your thought patterns, reassess challenges, and approach problems from different angles. It also enables you to remain open to new experiences and learning opportunities supporting your growth. By embracing new perspectives and solutions, you enhance your ability to cope with adversity and recover from setbacks more effectively.

Social Resilience

Social resilience is deeply connected to the support you receive from others. A network of family, friends, and loved ones who understand and support you provides emotional comfort, practical assistance, and a sense of belonging, all essential for resilience. Engaging with your social network can reduce feelings of isolation, boost your mood, and provide different perspectives on your challenges.

Additionally, consider having a professional support network that includes therapists, counselors, social workers, and medical professionals. Collaborating with professionals ensures comprehensive care and support, strengthening your resilience and fostering a more successful recovery.

Building resilience across emotional, physical, mental, and social domains creates a strong foundation for long-term recovery.

FUTURE-PROOFING YOUR RECOVERY

While emotional, physical, mental, and social resilience form the foundation of a vital recovery process, it is equally essential to future-proof your recovery by addressing the financial and legal aspects that can have long-term implications on your well-being. Ensuring you are financially and legally prepared can provide the stability and security needed to support your healing journey.

Main Steps for Financial Recovery

Besides the physical and emotional damage, a crash also leads to financial loss. The holistic recovery includes financial and legal recovery and healing other aspects of your well-being.

Below are the main steps for effective financial recovery:

Insurance Claims

After a crash, you must file your insurance claims promptly and ensure that all necessary documentation, such as medical reports, police reports, and repair estimates, are included. Be thorough in communicating with the insurance company, and do not hesitate to follow up if there are delays or issues. Effective insurance claims secure the financial resources needed to cover medical bills, lost wages, and other expenses, reducing the financial stress that can hinder your recovery.

Legal Representation

A lawyer specializing in personal injury or trauma cases can guide you through the complexities of legal proceedings. Legal representation can be equally significant if your case involves disputes with insurance companies, at-fault parties, or other entities. Your lawyer can negotiate settlements on your behalf, represent you in court if necessary, and advise you on the best course of action.

Document Your Expenses

Keeping detailed records of all your expenses related to the crash and your recovery facilitates financial and legal recovery. This includes medical bills, prescription costs, therapy sessions, transportation expenses, and any modifications to your home or lifestyle that are necessary due to your injuries.

Organized and accurate documentation can strengthen your position in negotiations with insurance companies or legal proceedings, ensuring you are adequately compensated for all your losses.

Main Steps for Legal Recovery

As discussed earlier in the book, a car crash may involve you in various legal matters. In addition to physical and mental recovery, you must also pursue legal action to accomplish your goal of holistic recovery.

Consult a Lawyer

The first step in legal recovery is to consult with a qualified lawyer. This initial consultation can provide you with an overview of your legal options and help you understand the potential outcomes of your case. Early legal consultation ensures you take the necessary steps to protect your rights and interests from the outset. This consultation lays the groundwork for a successful legal recovery.

Understand Your Rights

It is crucial to have a clear understanding of your legal rights following a traumatic event. This includes knowing your rights about insurance claims, compensation, medical care, and any legal actions that may be necessary. Understanding your rights empowers you to make informed decisions and avoid being taken advantage of by insurance companies, employers, or other parties involved in your case. Your lawyer can help explain these rights in detail and guide you through the legal processes that affect your recovery.

Active Participation

Active participation in your legal recovery process translates to staying engaged with your lawyer, keeping track of your case's progress, and proactively gathering and submitting required documentation or evidence. Your involvement can significantly influence the outcome of your case, as it ensures that all relevant information is presented and that your lawyer can build the strongest possible case on your behalf. Regular communication with your legal team, attending all necessary meetings or hearings, and promptly responding to any requests can help move your case forward efficiently and effectively.

These steps provide immediate relief and help ensure you have the resources and support necessary to continue building resilience in all areas of your life.

SURVIVOR STORIES

Below are some success stories of individuals who witnessed or experienced severe traffic crashes that altered their lives. However, they sought recovery and holistic healing, which transformed their lives.

Lisa Black's Survival Story

Lisa, a teacher at the University of Virginia Children's Hospital, was struck by a drunk driver on a typical October evening. She was on her way home from work when the crash altered her life. After being rushed back to the UVA Medical Center, she underwent several surgeries in the immediate hours following the crash. Lisa, who used to be a runner before the crash, suffered fractures in her neck, back, ribs, hands, legs, and knees — among other injuries.

When her orthopedic trauma surgeons asked about her goals and plans post-surgery, she clearly stated her plans to get back into her classroom as soon as possible. She also expressed her desire to get back into her running shoes again. Her surgeons were unsure about the possibility of executing these plans due to the severity of her injuries, but they did their best to provide her with the best care to facilitate her healing.

After undergoing intense surgeries and recovery treatments in the years following the crash, Lisa leveraged her strong willpower and accomplished her healing goals. She not only went back into the classroom but also started running again. It was all possible due to her commitment and dedication to her recovery.

Ben's Recovery Story

Ben is another trauma survivor whose life changed on a sunny Sunday morning. He got caught in a crash while on his motorbike. He remembers only stopping at a traffic signal and waking up on the road under a car. In the aftermath of the crash, several fractured bones and other severe injuries left him paralyzed from the waist down. Three years into recovery, he decided to revamp his life by not letting the crash and its impacts define his life and his future.

He acknowledged that there was still life beyond his crash and injuries; even if it was difficult, it was worth living and setting an example for others. To regain the sense of freedom he previously enjoyed, he mastered wheelchair tennis. Deciding to turn his injury into his strength, he even launched a social media app for disabled sports called Perfect Imperfections.

Zack's Survival and Recovery

Zack was only four years old and around three weeks away from his fifth birthday when a tragic crash altered the trajectory of his life. He remembers sleeping in his van on his way to church and waking up confused in a hospital. Soon, his diagnosis came, which revealed that he was paralyzed from the neck down due to a C-1 complete.

This was a huge blow for a child who had just started exploring the world and his life. However, he had the support of his mother, who told him that everything would turn out fine. While life threw several challenges at him after the crash, he soon realized that his mother was right. According to him, "Recovery was hard, especially as a child that just wanted to play all day rather than do therapy." However, with the support of his loved one and his willpower, Zack did not allow his disability to hinder his life. Even though he could not get back on his feet and deal with several complications that come with paralysis, he accepted and adapted to the new lifestyle. He said, "Life had its challenges, but with the help of God and my family, I've been able to live again, albeit differently, and live abundantly."

A SAMPLE TRAUMA RECOVERY AND RESILIENCE-BUILDING ACTION PLAN

Below is a sample trauma recovery and resilience-building action plan that you can tailor to your own needs and circumstances.

Physical Recovery

- **Objective:** Enhance physical health and regain strength and mobility.
- **Immediate Medical Care:** Follow through with all medical treatments and attend all scheduled appointments.
- **Physical Therapy:** Engage in physical therapy sessions as recommended by healthcare providers to restore movement and strength

- **Gentle Exercise:** Incorporate light exercises such as walking, stretching, and yoga, gradually increasing intensity based on comfort and medical advice
- Start with activities that do not strain the body, focusing on flexibility and muscle strengthening.

Emotional and Mental Well-being

- **Objective:** Improve emotional regulation and mental health.
- **Mindfulness and Meditation:** Practice mindfulness and meditation to reduce stress and anxiety. Begin with short sessions, gradually increasing the duration as comfort with the practice grows.
- **Professional Counseling:** Seek therapy or counseling to process emotional responses to the trauma.
- **Journaling:** Start a journal to express thoughts and feelings.

Social Support

- **Objective:** Build and maintain a supportive social network.
- **Family and Friends:** Regularly connect with family and friends.
- **Support Groups:** Join support groups for trauma survivors. Sharing experiences with others who have gone through similar situations.

Lifestyle Adjustments

- **Objective:** Adopt lifestyle changes that promote overall well-being.

- **Healthy Diet:** Focus on a balanced diet rich in nutrients that support recovery and energy levels.
- **Sleep Cycle:** Ensure adequate rest and establish a regular sleep schedule.
- **Limit Alcohol and Stimulants:** Reduce intake of alcohol and caffeine, as they can exacerbate anxiety and interfere with sleep patterns.

Skill Development

- **Objective:** Enhance skills that contribute to resilience and recovery.
- **Resilience Training:** Participate in resilience-building activities and exercises, including setting realistic goals, practicing gratitude, and learning to reframe negative thoughts into positive ones.
- **Adaptive Skills:** Work on developing adaptive skills such as problem-solving and decision-making.

Monitoring and Adjustment

- **Objective:** Regularly assess progress and make necessary adjustments to the action plan.
- **Self-Assessment:** Periodically evaluate physical, emotional, and mental state. Recognize achievements and identify areas that need more attention or a different approach.
- **Flexibility:** Be open to modifying the action plan based on recovery progress, challenges encountered, and changes in goals or needs.

Conclusion

Among various aftereffects of trauma, one is the reluctance to drive or ride in a car. After witnessing or experiencing a crash, you may have developed a fear of driving, refraining from returning to the road. I can understand how painful it can be to see others enjoying their road trips while you get flashbacks of your traumatic crash experience.

At the beginning of this journey, you might have been grappled with the fear of driving, but now that you have reached this point, I hope your fear would have been significantly reduced, if not eliminated.

The journey through this book has been one of healing, understanding, and reclaiming control. From acknowledging the impacts of a traffic crash on your body, mind, and spirit to exploring the healing options and discovering the long-term healing roadmap, we have come a long way.

Now, you can return to driving with less fear and more confidence. I also hope many of you have returned to the roads, reclaiming your lives and positively impacting those around you through advocacy and shared knowledge.

However, complete recovery is impossible without understanding that it is a process that goes beyond simply getting back behind the wheel. It is about managing anxiety, rebuilding your confidence, and restoring control over your life.

Recovery from the trauma of a traffic collision requires a comprehensive approach — one that is sensitive to your unique needs and experiences. This book has equipped you with the roadmap to walk this path and the tools you may need.

With trauma-informed traffic safety strategies, practical tools, and compassionate insights to overcome fear and anxiety related to driving, you can re-establish your sense of safety and independence on the road.

In the end, I want to reinforce the key takeaways of this book, which can be a part of your life:

- Recognizing that traffic crashes can cause significant emotional and psychological trauma is the first step toward recovery.
- Adopting trauma-informed strategies is crucial, ensuring that recovery methods are sensitive to the specific needs triggered by traffic crashes.
- Recovery is about comprehensive recovery that goes beyond just overcoming the fear of driving to include managing anxiety, rebuilding confidence, and restoring a sense of control over one's life.

Now, it is your turn. Take the wheel of your recovery! Apply the strategies you have learned, engage with your support network, and start reclaiming your confidence on the road. As discussed multiple times throughout the book, your journey may be bumpy and filled with unexpected challenges and setbacks. Expect to fall or stumble on your way, and be prepared to stand up, dust yourself off, and continue walking. Remember, the pace does not matter, and neither does the distance covered; the only thing that matters is your consistency. With persistence and the right tools, you can overcome obstacles and move forward with strength.

Several success stories mentioned in this book offer the lessons of consistency, resilience, and commitment to your goal. While their stories and experiences might differ, one thing is common among them—starting small, sticking to the journey, and trusting the process.

Instead of going all out, you can begin with small steps, for instance, seeking therapy and counseling, beginning with short drives around the block and eventually progressing to longer journeys. During all these steps, the encouragement of your support network is crucial.

Moreover, once you overcome your trauma, anxiety, and fear, you can empower others by sharing your knowledge and experience with others. Real freedom and independence empower and uplift others around you.

Finally, if you found value in this book, I encourage you to share your thoughts by leaving a review. Several other trauma survivors like you might be looking for help. Your feedback can help others on a similar journey find the support and guidance they need. You have proved your resilience and commitment to self-care by taking this vital step towards healing and reclaiming your life. I wish you the best for leveraging this new beginning to improve your life.

RESOURCE LINKS & QR CODES

OVERVIEW

Links	QR Codes
https://www.ncbi.nlm.nih.gov/pmc/articles/PMC8141461/	
https://www.nsvrc.org/blogs/exploring-conversation-trauma-blog-series/Glossary	
https://www.complextrauma.org/glossary/	

INTRODUCTION

Links	QR Codes
https://www.ncbi.nlm.nih.gov/pmc/articles/PMC2396820/	
https://www.apa.org/news/press/releases/2003/12/accidents-ptsd	
https://www.ncbi.nlm.nih.gov/pmc/articles/PMC3256803/	

CHAPTER 1

Links	QR Codes
https://www.coastallightcounseling.com/single-post/complex-nature-of-trauma	
https://familypsychnj.com/2019/02/the-nature-of-trauma-and-its-effect-on-the-ptsd-brain/	
https://www.ncbi.nlm.nih.gov/pmc/articles/PMC3181584/	
https://www.verywellmind.com/trauma-therapy-definition-types-techniques-and-efficacy-5191413	
https://www.lawinfo.com/resources/car-accident/how-car-accidents-affect-your-mental-health.html	

https://www.boohofflaw.com/ptsd-car-accident/	
https://dominguezfirm.com/injury-lawyer/car-accident/the-emotional-impact-of-car-accidents/	
https://traumainformedoregon.org/resources/new-to-trauma-informed-care/trauma-informed-care- principles/	
https://www.cdc.gov/orr/infographics/6_principles_trauma_info.htm	
https://www.betterhealth.vic.gov.au/health/healthyliving/trauma-and-families	

https://www.umassglobal.edu/news-and-events/blog/trauma-informed-care-for-helping-professionals	
https://www.ncbi.nlm.nih.gov/pmc/articles/PMC10701293/	
https://www.ncbi.nlm.nih.gov/books/NBK207192/	
https://adaa.org/learn-from-us/from-the-experts/blog-posts/consumer/how-cope-trauma-after-accident	
https://www.betterhealth.vic.gov.au/health/conditionsandtreatments/trauma-reaction-and-recovery	

https://www.brake.org.uk/how-we-help/get-help-if-a-crash-victim/information-and-advice-after-road-death-or-serious-injury/serious-injury-in-a-road-crash/section-7-coping-with-shock-and-emotions-and-getting-support

CHAPTER 2

Links	QR Codes
https://www.rmlawcall.com/the-psychological-effects-of-car-accidents-on-bystanders-and-witnesses	
https://www.claimsaction.co.uk/the-psychological-impact-of-car-accidents-on-drivers-and-passengers/	
https://adaa.org/learn-from-us/from-the-experts/blog-posts/consumer/how-cope-trauma-after-accident	
https://www.mind.org.uk/information-support/types-of-mental-health-problems/trauma/coping-with- trauma/	
https://www.verywellmind.com/emotional-shock-definition-symptoms-causes-and-treatment-5214434	

https://www.cigna.com/knowledge-center/witnessing-a-traumatic-event	
https://adaa.org/learn-from-us/from-the-experts/blog-posts/consumer/how-cope-trauma-after-accident	
https://www.enjuris.com/personal-injury/emotional-recovery-after-accident/	
https://www.bankrate.com/insurance/car/trauma-from-car-accidents/	
https://camllp.com/2020/09/21/four-steps-to-coping-after-a-car-accident/	

https://www.johnfoy.com/faqs/what-should-i-do-in-the-days-following-a-car-accident/	
https://kidshealth.org/en/teens/post-crash.html	
https://nelliganlaw.ca/blog/6-steps-follow-motor-vehicle-accident/	

CHAPTER 3

Links	QR Codes
https://www.ncbi.nlm.nih.gov/pmc/articles/PMC9165651/	
https://bmcpsychiatry.biomedcentral.com/articles/10.1186/s12888-018-1680-4	
https://www.claimsaction.co.uk/the-psychological-impact-of-car-accidents-on-drivers-and-passengers/	
https://www.kraftlaw.com/legal-articles/how-car-accidents-can-cause-post-traumatic-stress-disorder/	
https://www.mayoclinic.org/diseases-conditions/post-traumatic-stress-disorder/symptoms-causes/syc- 20355967	

https://www.psychiatry.org/patients-families/ptsd/what-is-ptsd

https://www.healthline.com/health/somatic-experiencing

https://www.ncbi.nlm.nih.gov/pmc/articles/PMC5518443/

https://traumahealing.org/se-101/

https://psychcentral.com/lib/somatic-therapy-exercises-for-trauma

https://www.charliehealth.com/post/somatic-exercises-for-mental-health	
https://psychcentral.com/health/what-is-trauma-informed-yoga	
https://kripalu.org/resources/how-yoga-helps-heal-trauma-qa-bessel-van-der-kolk	
https://www.verywellmind.com/abdominal-breathing-2584115	
https://www.jmu.edu/counselingctr/self-help/anxiety/controlled-breathing.shtml	

https://www.ryandelaney.co/blog/somatic-breathwork	
https://psychcentral.com/health/what-is-trauma-informed-yoga	
https://khironclinics.com/blog/trauma-informed-tai-chi/	
https://www.meditationmag.com/blog/7-tips-for-healing-trauma-through-meditation/	
https://adaa.org/learn-from-us/from-the-experts/blog-posts/consumer/how-cope-trauma-after-accident	

https://www.charliehealth.com/post/somatic-exercises-for-mental-health	
https://wellnessdripholyoke.com/breathing-techniques-grounding-exercises-ptsd/	
https://www.everydayhealth.com/emotional-health/somatic-therapy/	
https://www.firstsession.com/resources/somatic-therapy-exercises-techniques	
https://positivepsychology.com/somatic-experiencing/	

CHAPTER 4

Links	QR Codes
https://www.kentuckycourage.com/blog/how-to-mentally-recover-from-a-car-accident/	
https://www.carranza.on.ca/resources/blog-post/personal-injury-blog/2022/05/20/deal-post-traumatic-stress-disorder-after-vehicular-accident	
https://www.kentuckycourage.com/blog/how-to-mentally-recover-from-a-car-accident/	
https://www.nationwide.com/lc/resources/auto-insurance/articles/driving-safety-tips	
https://www.linkedin.com/pulse/how-make-sure-your-car-safe-drive-road-sydur-rahman	

https://flteensafedriver.org/72-safe-driving-tips-that-could-save-your-life/	
https://roadguardians.org/overcoming-your-fear-of-riding-after-a-motorcycle-accident/	
https://www.leithtoyota.com/blogs/1483/safety/4-tips-regaining-confidence-car-accident/	
https://www.knowyourrights.com/blog/how-to-overcome-the-fear-of-driving-after-an-accident/	
https://www.murphys-law.com.au/blog/regain-confidence-after-car-accident/	

https://www.utires.com/articles/safe-driving-app/	
https://www.nsc.org/safety-training/defensive-driving/nsc-defensive-driving-courses	
https://www.government-fleet.com/10143195/the-4-principles-of-safe-driving	
https://www.safetyconnect.io/post/10-point-driving-safety-checklist-for-organizations	
https://www.saif.com/safety-and-health/topics/prevent-injuries/safe-driving.html	

https://www.nationwide.com/lc/resources/auto-insurance/articles/driving-safety-tips	
https://www.nhtsa.gov/vehicle-safety/driver-assistance-technologies	
https://www.choosingtherapy.com/ptsd-after-car-accident/	
https://www.axa.com.ph/multimedia/articles/back-to-basics-of-road-safety-defense-driving	
https://www.marsalisilaw.com/how-to-drive-with-confidence-again-after-being-involved-in-an-accident/	

https://blog.drivedifferent. com/blog/7-tips-for-overcomin g-driving-anxiety-after-a-crash	
https://living.geico.com/driving/ auto/car-safety-insurance/ tips-for-driving-again-after-an-accident/	
https://www.injuredcalltoday.com/9-steps-t o-regain-confidence-after-a-car-accident/	
https://www.trollingerlaw.com/ car-accident-lawyer/what-to-do/	
https://www.nhtsa.gov/road-safety/ driving-in-severe-weather	

https://kidshealth.org/en/teens/driving-conditions.html	
https://www.jdpower.com/cars/shopping-guides/safety-tips-for-driving-in-bad-weather	
https://www.cheshirefire.gov.uk/your-safety/road-safety/using-roads-safely/driving-in-adverse-weather/	

CHAPTER 5

Links	QR Codes
https://www.jamiecasinoinjuryattorneys.com/in-the-news/2023/october/the-emotional-impact-of-car-accidents-coping-and/	
https://www.pinderplotkin.com/car-accident-recovery/	
https://www.payaslaw.com/the-importance-of-seeking-psychological-treatment-after-a-car-accident/	
https://www.ncbi.nlm.nih.gov/pmc/articles/PMC4490643/	
https://fastercapital.com/topics/finding-the-right-support-group-for-you.html	

https://www.homehealthcompanions.com/finding-the-right-support-group/	
https://www.mayoclinic.org/healthy-lifestyle/stress-management/in-depth/support-groups/art-20044655	
https://www.heretohelp.bc.ca/infosheet/choosing-a-support-group-thats-right-for-you	
https://accidentcarechiropractic.com/family-and-friends-supporting-loved-ones-after-an-auto-accident/	
https://spokanechristiancounseling.com/articles/understanding-and-coping-with-trauma-the-impact-of-car-accidents	

https://www.gjel.com/blog/how-to-support-an-acciden t-victim-tips-for-friends-and-family	
https://www.smithandhassler.com/articles/doctors-treat-car-accident-injuries/	
https://www.fosterwallace.com/blog/medical-attention-after-a-car-accident.cfm	
https://mvamvp.com/how-a-trauma-counselor-can-hel p-you-after-a-motor-accident/	
https://farahandfarah.com/traumatic-accidents-mental-health/	

https://wolfandpravato.com/can-a-car-accident-lawyer-help-with-emotional-and-psychological- damages/	
https://www.findlaw.com/injury/car-accidents/get-legal-help-with-a-motor-vehicle-accident.html	
https://www.sargonlawgroup.com/your-guide-to-charities-and-free-programs-for-car-accident-victims/	
https://crashsupportnetwork.com/online-support/	
https://www.crlegalteam.com/car-accidents/auto-accident-resources/	

https://farahandfarah.com/traumatic-accidents-mental-health/	
https://madd.org/	
https://www.iihs.org/	
https://unitedspinal.org/peer-support-groups/	
https://www.amputee-coalition.org/support-groups-peer-support/support-group-network/	

https://www.biausa.org/public-affairs/media/virtual-support-groups	
https://www.roadpeace.org/	
https://www.mydenverinjurylawyer.com/motorcycle-accident-support-groups/	
https://www.samhsa.gov/find-help/disaster-distress-helpline/coping-tips	
https://www.enjuris.com/personal-injury/emotional-recovery-after-accident/	

CHAPTER 6

Links	QR Codes
https://www.apa.org/ptsd-guideline/patients-and-families/cognitive-behavioral	
https://psychcentral.com/pro/the-basic-principles-of-cognitive-behavior-therapy	
https://www.mindmypeelings.com/blog/cbt-principles	
https://my.clevelandclinic.org/health/treatments/21208-cognitive-behavioral-therapy-cbt	
https://cogbtherapy.com/cognitive-behavior-therapy-techniques	

https://www.verywellmind.com/what-is-cognitive-behavior-therapy-2795747	
https://www.ncbi.nlm.nih.gov/pmc/articles/PMC2396820/	
https://www.ncbi.nlm.nih.gov/pmc/articles/PMC1393456/	
https://www.truthlegal.com/how-cbt-can-help-after-a-road-traffic-accident/	
https://www.aheadpsych.com.au/driving-anxiety/	

https://www.aheadpsych.com.au/driving-anxiety/	
https://en.wikipedia.org/wiki/Exposure_therapy	
https://www.webmd.com/mental-health/what-is-exposure-therapy	
https://www.apa.org/ptsd-guideline/patients-and-families/exposure-therapy	
https://www.forbes.com/health/mind/exposure-therapy/	

https://www.linkedin.com/pulse/holistic-approach-real-exposure-therapy-ptsd-related-motor-naser	
https://www.ncbi.nlm.nih.gov/pmc/articles/PMC3433579/	
https://pubmed.ncbi.nlm.nih.gov/17292693/	
https://pubmed.ncbi.nlm.nih.gov/17292693/	
https://www.sciencedirect.com/science/article/abs/pii/S0005789406000670	

https://www.ncbi.nlm.nih.gov/pmc/articles/
PMC9006570/

https://www.sciencedirect.com/science/
article/abs/pii/S0272735821001586

https://psychcentral.com/health/
emdr-therapy

https://mysydneypsychologist.
com.au/how-does-emdr-work-
a-neuroscience-explanation/

https://www.frontiersin.org/journals/
psychology/articles/10.3389/
fpsyg.2017.01935/full

https://www.ncbi.nlm.nih.gov/pmc/articles/PMC4404810/	
https://www.psychiatria-danubina.com/UserDocsImages/pdf/dnb_vol33_sup1/dnb_vol33_sup1_88.pdf	
https://www.frontiersin.org/journals/psychology/articles/10.3389/fpsyg.2022.845481/full	
https://www.ncbi.nlm.nih.gov/pmc/articles/PMC9896113/	
https://www.ptsd.va.gov/gethelp/selfhelp_coping.asp	

https://www.ncbi.nlm.nih.gov/pmc/articles/PMC4849385/	
https://www.helpguide.org/articles/ptsd-trauma/ptsd-symptoms-self-help-treatment.htm	
https://deltadiscoverycenter.com/trauma-therapy-techniques-help-you-heal-from-trauma/	
https://www.verywellmind.com/10-ways-to-heal-from-trauma-5206940#toc-practice-mindfulness-or- meditation	
https://deltadiscoverycenter.com/trauma-therapy-techniques-help-you-heal-from-trauma/	

https://seattleanxiety.com/psychiatrist/2022/7/12/ptsd-self-care-tips	
https://seattleanxiety.com/psychiatrist/2022/7/12/ptsd-self-care-tips	
https://positivepsychology.com/cbt/	
https://www.psychologytools.com/self-help/what-is-cbt/	
https://www.healthline.com/health/cbt-techniques	

CHAPTER 7

Links	QR Codes
https://www.gracetherapyaustin.com/post/why-routine-is-important-in-healing-trauma	
https://www.verywellmind.com/the-importance-of-keeping-a-routine-during-stressful-times-4802638	
https://fortbehavioral.com/addiction-recovery-blog/the-importance-of-routines/	
https://firstaccessbh.org/blog/routinesandptsd	
https://www.frontiersin.org/articles/10.3389/fnbeh.2022.829571/full	

https://www.ticti.org/exercise/	
https://www.ncbi.nlm.nih.gov/pmc/articles/PMC10158556/	
https://www.helpguide.org/articles/ptsd-trauma/coping-with-emotional-and-psychological-trauma.htm	
https://www.frontiersin.org/articles/10.3389/fnbeh.2022.829571/full	
https://www.frontiersin.org/journals/psychology/articles/10.3389/fpsyg.2023.1215250/full	

https://www.phoenixaustralia.org/disaster-hub/toolkits/physical-activity/	
https://www.ncbi.nlm.nih.gov/pmc/articles/PMC10400004/	
https://health.clevelandclinic.org/trauma-informed-yoga	
https://www.frontiersin.org/articles/10.3389/fnbeh.2022.829571/full	
https://www.innisintegrativetherapy.com/blog/2017/5/2/how-exercise-helps-your-brain-heal-after- trauma	

https://www.sciencedirect.com/science/article/pii/S175529662300073X

https://stylesagascope.com.in/the-healing-benefits-of-mindful-movement-practices-alexander-technique-feldenkrais-and-somatic-experiencing-for-trauma-recovery/

https://psychcentral.com/health/what-is-trauma-informed-yoga

https://psychcentral.com/health/trauma-informed-mindfulness

https://www.medicalnewstoday.com/articles/the-connection-between-post-traumatic-stress-disorder-and-nutrition

https://www.onlymyhealth.
com/nutrients-essential-for-pos
t-trauma-recovery-1698219269

https://www.webmd.com/mental-health/
news/20231023/mediterranean-diet-linke
d-fewer-ptsd- symptoms-study

https://www.sleepfoundation.org/
mental-health/ptsd-and-sleep

https://www.ptsd.va.gov/understand/
related/sleep_problems.asp

https://www.healthline.com/health/
mental-health/trauma-recovery

https://tinybuddha.com/blog/how-a-simple-morning-routine-helped-me-heal-from-ptsd-and-grief/	
https://www.theguesthouseocala.com/simple-routines-to-combat-trauma/	
https://leisurelifelinelens.com.in/the-healing-benefits-of-mindful-movement-for-trauma-survivors- trauma-informed-yoga-dance-movement-therapy-and-body-oriented-psychotherapy/	
https://tarrant.tx.networkofcare.org/kids/library/article.aspx?id=376	
https://realpsychiatricservices.com/ptsd-altering-your-lifestyle.html	

https://www.betterhealth.vic.gov. au/health/conditionsandtreatments/ anxiety-treatment-options	
https://vancouveremdrtherapy. com/routines-for-helping-cope-wit h-ptsd-and-other-emotional-stressors/	
https://www.takingcharge.csh. umn.edu/what-lifestyle-changes-ar e-recommended-anxiety-and- depression	
https://www.healthline.com/health/ natural-ways-to-reduce-anxiety#anxiety- treatment	

CHAPTER 8

Links	QR Codes
https://www.aftertrauma.org/symptoms-and-difficulties-after-trauma/symptoms-and-difficulties-after- trauma	
https://www.brightquest.com/post-traumatic-stress-disorder/retraumatization/	
https://www.brightquest.com/post-traumatic-stress-disorder/retraumatization/	
https://michaelgquirke.com/what-to-do-after-a-setback-in-trauma-healing/	
https://www.therapycincinnati.com/blog/how-to-deal-with-setbacks-in-trauma-healing	

https://www.brightquest.com/post-traumatic-stress-disorder/retraumatization/	
https://www.therapycincinnati.com/blog/how-to-deal-with-setbacks-in-trauma-healing	
https://www.healthline.com/health/mental-health/trauma-recovery	
https://www.healthyplace.com/blogs/recoveringfrommentalillness/2022/11/resilience-in-mental-health-recovery-dealing-with-setbacks	
https://www.kolmac.com/navigating-setbacks-on-your-substance-use-recovery-journey-five-strategies-for-resilience/	

https://blackhorsehealth.com/treatment-plans-goals-and-objectives-for-trauma/

https://mentalhealth.vermont.gov/services/adult-mental-health-services/recovery/ten-components- recovery

https://www.linkedin.com/pulse/5-essential-healing-components-trauma-therapy-joe-rabiega

https://mentalhealth.vermont.gov/services/adult-mental-health-services/recovery/ten-components- recovery

https://relevancerecovery.com/blog/how-to-deal-with-triggers-from-trauma/

https://stepsforchange.us/
types-of-trauma-triggers/

https://www.webmd.com/mental-health/
what-are-ptsd-triggers

CHAPTER 9

Links	QR Codes
https://www.linkedin.com/advice/1/how-can-you-leverage-different-platforms-formats	
https://www.southpacificprivate.com.au/our-blog/family-friends/how-to-respond-when-someone- discloses-trauma/	
https://www.sneedmitchell.com/post/what-do-you-say-to-someone-who-survived-a-bad-car-crash	
https://www.linkedin.com/advice/1/how-can-you-handle-negative-feedback-your-storytelling-jxcse	
https://www.wattpad.com/855187-inside-scoop-2-dealing-with-negative-comments	

https://buffer.com/resources/social-media-negativity/	
https://bootcamp.uxdesign.cc/overcoming-negative-feedback-social-media-criticism-53d30987619e	
https://www.ncbi.nlm.nih.gov/pmc/articles/PMC387488/	
https://www.hsestudyguide.com/10-importance-of-road-safety/#google_vignette	
https://www.aa-namibia.com/road-safety-advocacy/	

https://www.who.int/activities/advocating-for-road-safety	
https://www.unicef.org/blog/meaningfully-engaging-with-youth-on-road-safety	
https://www.marylandinjurylawyer.net/importance-of-driver-awareness-to-traffic-safety.html	
https://wechope.org/our-stories/4-key-ways-sharing-your-story-makes-a-difference-and-tips-for-telling/	
https://www.linkedin.com/pulse/should-you-sharing-personal-stories-social-media-dante-st-james	

https://drivingintherealworld.com/
dawne-mckay-of-crash-support-network/

https://ncsacw.acf.hhs.gov/userfiles/files/
SAMHSA_Trauma.pdf

https://www.pacesconnection.
com/fileSendAction/fcType/5/
fcOid/531493897488254290/
fodoid/531493897488254286/ATSP%
20Brief_FINAL.pdf

https://www.advocacyincubator.org/
program-areas/injury-prevention/
road-safety

https://cifal.up.edu.ph/
advocacy-and-outreach/road-safety/

https://ndaa.org/programs/ntlc/other-traffic-and-safety-partners/	
https://www.ghsa.org/about/associate-members/issue-advocacy	

CHAPTER 10

Links	QR Codes
https://www.choosingtherapy.com/ptsd-after-car-accident/	
https://www.braininjurylawofseattle.com/ptsd-after-car-accident/	
https://www.ncbi.nlm.nih.gov/pmc/articles/PMC2396820/	
https://www.pinderplotkin.com/ptsd-and-car-accidents/	
https://blog.yeghip.com/bouncing-back-how-psychology-can-help-you-heal-after-a-car-crash	

https://www.lazzaralegal.com/attorney-profile/our-blog/2024/january/how-to-take-care-of-your-mental-health-after-a-c/	
https://www.choosingtherapy.com/ptsd-after-car-accident/	
https://southvanphysio.com/car-accident-physical-therapy/	
https://www.pinderplotkin.com/car-accident-recovery/	
https://www.procaremedcenter.com/car-accident-recovery-a-full-guide-to-faster-healing/	

https://www.lazzaralegal.com/attorney-profile/our-blog/2024/january/how-to-take-care-of-your-mental-health-after-a-c/

https://hqlo.biomedcentral.com/articles/10.1186/s12955-015-0291-8

https://revivalottawa.com/how-a-social-worker-can-help-after-a-motor-vehicle-accident/

https://resslertesh.com/future-damages-for-pain-suffering/

https://www.callahan-law.com/financial-recovery-after-catastrophe-maximizing-compensation-for-severe-injuries/

https://shinerlawgroup.com/what-type-of-damages-can-you-recover-after-a-car-accident/	
https://shinerlawgroup.com/what-type-of-damages-can-you-recover-after-a-car-accident/	
https://resslertesh.com/future-damages-for-pain-suffering/	
https://www.traumasurvivorsnetwork.org/pages/survivor-stories	
https://www.aftertrauma.org/survivors-stories/survivors-stories	

https://www.apa.org/topics/
disasters-response/recovering

https://physiciansgroupllc.com/a-guide-t
o-recovery-after-auto-accidents/

Made in the USA
Columbia, SC
08 January 2025